Any one can Bake

Compiled by the Educational Department
of the
ROYAL BAKING POWDER CO.
100 East 42 nd St. New York City

Any One Can Bake—*Index to Recipes*

Foreword

To one person it is given to take brushes and colors and so combine them that there is produced a work of art. To another is given the ability to set down the melody lying in his imagination so that when it is played there comes forth music which is called a masterpiece.

Just as paints and oils and musical notes are all about us, so there are, at every hand, wide varieties of food products which one may fashion into dishes which, too, are works of art.

In the cottage kitchen and in the kitchen of the great house upon the hill, there is equal facility for producing foods which combine pleasing appearance with exquisite flavor.

In a book so modest in size, we have deemed it best to try to do one thing well and so have confined ourselves to some of the delightful dishes produced by baking. Then, realizing the importance of the proper serving of delicious foods, we have given adequate space to this interesting feature.

Going one step further, it follows that under varying conditions and for different groups of people, the same dish takes on different aspects when served in combination with other dishes. So time has been taken to discuss combinations of foods in which each dish fits and blends into a composite menu of unusual taste and balance.

It is our hope that this book may be taken into a quiet corner for sincere reading. It should prove as interesting as the newest romance because what is more fascinating than the secret of producing unusual dishes and serving them daintily and appropriately?

As one reads this book, it will be found that many of those things which have puzzled the housewife and which have been considered intricate and only to be undertaken by experts, are explained step by step and illustrated so plainly that even the inexperienced housewife will find them not only really simple to make but very enjoyable to produce.

Before this book was ready to print, each recipe and each suggestion was tested and proved. Years of experience on the part of those who love and appreciate the fine art of cooking have gone into each page. It will be found expedient to follow them carefully and accurately.

As you read, you will find that students of cooking have made some wonderful discoveries. In the fine art of cookery, there are certain basic laws. They teach that at the bottom of the art of baking there lie but a few "master" recipes. Like the fundamental laws of painting and music, they are founded upon simplicity and harmony.

These "master" recipes are susceptible to many variations, many of which are developed and illustrated in the pages which follow. Once you have learned even one or two of them, you are able to set forth a score or more of appealing and intriguing dishes as simple to make as they will prove enjoyable to serve.

Table Appointments
and Table Service . .

SO much of the enjoyment of a meal depends upon the attractiveness of its service that a charming table is almost as important as good food.

And what woman does not take pleasure in pretty linen, spotlessly clean; shining silver, glass and china?

Fortunately, our desire for an attractive table is easy to indulge these days, when really delightful things may be had so inexpensively.

Tables

There are any number of attractive tables from which to choose—round, square, oblong, oval and the long refectory tables.

The oblong table is perhaps most popular at present, and it does lend itself most admirably to the serving of formal meals.

For the small and intimate meal the new tea wagons that can be opened out for a luncheon for two or even four are most convenient. Nests of coffee tables are convenient, too, and useful for the buffet supper in the small apartment.

All these tables can be had in various woods and finishes, but should be selected with an idea of their appropriateness and should, of course, be in keeping with other furnishings.

Tables must be kept well polished with any of the good furniture oils on the market and should be protected from the heat of hot dishes with felt or asbestos pads.

Cloths

The white damask cloth with hand-hemmed or hemstitched napkins to match is correct for any meal and is generally used for the formal dinner unless a very handsome lace cloth is available. Centerpieces are occasionally used with damask cloths, but are not necessary, as the pattern of a beautiful cloth is generally preferred.

Cloths in tinted damask or with colored borders are attractive and are now used a great deal for both the family breakfast and for the more informal luncheon party. How-

ever, for the formal service these cloths are not as correct as the plain damask.

Various shades of cream linen, shading almost to ecru, either plain or with hems embroidered in color, are good for the informal breakfast, luncheon or supper and can be purchased at moderate prices. Luncheon sets of bright colored two-toned plaid linen are especially pretty for the cottage or kitchenette table.

Doilies and runners or scarfs are correct for any meal with the exception of the formal dinner.

One long runner down the middle of the table with square or oblong mat at each cover, or two long runners down either side with centerpiece and end mats, or centerpiece with doilies on a nicely polished table are all correct and very much used.

Two long runners down either side are usually used for the refectory table, and for special occasions the Italian and Spanish lace cloths are lovely and effective.

The important points to remember are to have the sets match, to have only sufficient to preserve your table and to have them in keeping with the other table appointments.

A large doily for each cover, small ones for the butter plate and the glass and where oblong mats are used, one for each cover are all that are necessary.

Silence cloths of felt or asbestos are always used under the damask cloth.

Whether damask, linen or lace, the table cloths, doilies, runners, centerpieces and napkins should never be starched and should be spotlessly clean and most carefully laundered, with few if any folds. Doilies, runners and centerpieces are never folded but rolled on cardboard kept for this purpose.

Napkins

Napkins should always match the cloth and with a plain hand-hemmed damask cloth only hand-hemmed napkins should be used. For breakfast, luncheon or supper, the eighteen-inch square napkin; for dinner either the twenty or twenty-two-inch, and for the formal dinner the very large twenty-seven-inch napkin is correct.

Table Decorations

Individual taste, of course, decides the matter of table decorations and keeps them in harmony with the other table appointments and with the spirit of the occasion.

Flowers may be arranged in floats, bowls or vases of pottery, glass, china or silver. They are usually more effective if loosely arranged, very much as they grow, so each blossom with its leaves can show how lovely it is.

Don't forget that the stems and leaves are often as decorative as the blossoms.

The ophelia or butterfly rose with delphinium, lavender laces and white baby's breath or stevia—a few sprays of each in a glass float are lovely. Larkspur, sweet peas and sweet alyssum also make a pretty combination.

Roses by themselves are prettier than when combined with asparagus ferns, though the latter are very good with carnations, chrysanthemums, and any flower that does not possess as beautiful a stem as the rose.

Reds and yellows, or blues and reds do not usually make pleasing combinations; neither do browns and bright pinks, except perhaps in the case of zinias. Here the riot of color in browns, pinks, yellows, reds and orange offers a most striking centerpiece in certain settings.

Fruit well arranged in a bowl or a basket is appropriate for breakfast or even for the formal dinner, and its beautiful bright colors add greatly to the festiveness of the autumn or winter table.

Candles and tall thin tapers, are used without shades in any of the many varieties of candlesticks or candelabra now available and are appropriate for dinner, afternoon tea or supper. The colors most useful are deep ivory tones and gold.

China will vary in color and elaborateness to suit the personal taste. While complete sets are always in vogue, service plates, salad and dessert plates of a different pattern can be used and are correct.

Glass for the table changes almost with each year and many of the modern tables are set with delicately tinted glass. Plain white crystal is always in good taste, but the colored Mexican, Spanish, and Venetian glass can be used on almost any table if appropriately combined with china and other furnishings.

Silver for the table will be in accord with other appointments and there are many beautiful standard patterns in both solid and plated silver from which to choose.

A refectory table with deep ecru hemstitched linen runner and mats, brass candlesticks, Italian or Spanish pottery dishes, and tinted glass tumblers, with fruit as the centerpiece is an attractive and well-appointed supper table.

Table Service

The cloth is placed with center fold exactly down the center of the table, centerpiece exactly in center, and candlesticks placed the same distance on either side of the centerpiece. All the covers or places are set the same distance apart. Napkins are folded once in half lengthwise or in three folds where monogrammed, or they are laid flat and unfolded. They are placed at the left of the cover and one inch from the table edge or on the service plate. Silver is laid one inch from the edge of the table. Forks are placed at the left. Knives, with sharp edges turned in, and spoons are placed at the right.

Each must be placed in the order of use, that is, the first to be used is farthest from the plate. The butter plate with butter knife is always at the upper left corner and the glass at the upper right corner of each place. Salads served with the main course are always placed at the left of the cover and cups and saucers at the right.

A service plate should be at each place before the meal is served and it remains on the table until after the soup. Glasses should be three-quarters filled just before sitting down at the table.

All serving and placing of food is from the left of the person to be served, with the exception of beverages. All dishes must be removed from the left with the exception of glasses and cups and saucers. The table is cleared and crumbs are removed just before the dessert.

Finger bowls are placed before the course for which they are needed and always before dessert. The bowl is placed on a doily on the dessert plate and each guest removes the doily with the bowl as dessert is served.

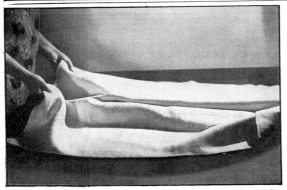

1 If damask cloth is to be used, cover table with silence cloth made of felt or with a bound asbestos pad made to fit your table.

2 Lay cloth exactly in center of table allowing it to hang at least twelve inches over edge of table. Cloth may be folded, but a center design shows better without folds.

5 Place forks at the left and knives, with blades turned in, at the right, one inch from edge of table. Place spoons at right in order of use, cocktail spoon at outside, consommé spoon next to knife.

6 Either teaspoon or bouillon spoon is correct for the consommé. Place napkin at left of fork; butter plate at upper left at tip of fork with butter knife on plate. Place glasses at upper right.

9 For breakfast, luncheon, supper or even for the formal dinner, runners and doilies may be used instead of the damask cloth. Asbestos mats are placed under each place if hot dishes are to be served.

10 Fruit, instead of flowers, makes a most attractive table decoration, and is very appropriate with these Italian runners and Wedgewood china.

3 Place flowers or other decoration next. Silver or glass candlesticks would be appropriate with this centerpiece but for an informal luncheon they are seldom used.

4 Setting table for this luncheon: *Fruit-Mint Cocktail, Consommé, Royal Luncheon Rolls, Fried Chicken, Peas, Hominy Croquettes, Ice Cream Puffs, Demi-Tasse.*

7 Place salts and peppers between two guests and a service plate in center of each place. Remove service plate with consommé and substitute a hot plate with the chicken. Vegetables and hot rolls are passed. Coffee is served in the drawing-room.

8 Just before luncheon, place butter on plates, fill glasses, place cocktail. Remove salts and peppers, butter plates and crumbs before dessert. The finger bowls and plates with silver are placed for dessert.

11 For an informal meal, the dessert may be served at the table. Silver for serving is placed in front of the hostess. Individual dessert fork and spoon are put at each place before the plates and the dessert are set before the hostess.

12 Table laid for a formal luncheon: *Oysters, Celery, Olives, Consommé Julienne, Rolls, Roast Duck, Apple Stuffing, Grape Jelly, Spinach Soufflé, Riced Potatoes, Escarole, Paprika Dressing, Toasted Wafers, Royal Chocolate Pudding, Foamy Sauce, Spiced Almonds, Coffee, Cream Mints.*

Various Ingredients used in Royal Baking Powder recipes

Flours

There are two kinds of flour generally used in baking, bread or all-purpose flour and pastry or cake flour. Unless otherwise specified, the flour indicated in Royal recipes means bread flour milled from spring wheat. Bread flour contains more gluten and is best for breads, rolls and biscuits. It is also satisfactory for cakes. For those who prefer a fluffier and more delicate biscuit or cake, pastry flour, which is milled from winter wheat and which contains more starch, may be used. Use pastry flour in same proportions as bread flour, and always sift flour before measuring, and again with the baking powder. Cakes made with pastry flour are better eaten the day they are made, as they do not keep as moist as those made with bread flour.

For a home-made pastry flour substitute for two tablespoons bread flour in each cup of flour, one tablespoon cornstarch and mix thoroughly.

Flours such as potato, rice, corn, rye, whole wheat, graham and buckwheat, are also used in quick breads and, in a few instances, in cakes. Each can be used as the only flour in a recipe but generally they produce more attractive results when combined with wheat flour. The usual proportion is one part wheat flour to two parts other flour or half and half. Potato and rice flours require more liquid; they cannot be substituted for wheat flour without changing amounts of other ingredients.

Potato flour makes an excellent sponge cake; use half the amount called for in an ordinary wheat flour recipe.

Meals

Corn meal, rye meal, graham meal, oatmeal (ground), and bran are excellent for Boston Brown Bread and other coarse flour breads. They should be mixed with other dry ingredients without sifting, as their great dietetic value lies in their husks or bran coats. Coarse meals and flours are not only wholesome and appetizing but give many pleasant variations to the menu.

Shortening

Shortening is butter, lard, oil or other fat used in cooking. Use a good leaf lard or substitute for breads, rolls, pastry and biscuits, or part lard and part butter, or butter substitute. Use butter or butter substitute in cakes, with the exception of molasses cake or gingerbread, where lard may be used. Butter, because of its flavor, is generally recommended for cakes, butter icings and fillings. For white cakes a white shortening is often preferred.

Vegetable cooking oils are excellent for bread and may also be used in cakes and pastries, but they should be used in lesser amounts than solid shortening and combined with other ingredients differently. Since most of the cooking oils are unsalted, salt should be added.

Olive Oil, delicious in salad dressings and for frying, is not satisfactory for cakes.

Sugar

Granulated or Castor Sugar in English recipes is intended where simply sugar is mentioned. It is best for breads and cakes and boiled icing. For cakes of fine texture a very fine granulated sugar is recommended, or ordinary sugar sifted two or three times.

Powdered Sugar makes a fine-grained cake but one that will dry out quickly. When substituted for granulated sugar, it produces a cake slightly less sweet. It is excellent for lady fingers, pound cake and cottage pudding.

Confectioner's or XXXX Sugar or Icing Sugar is used for uncooked frostings and fillings. It combines readily with liquid making a smooth, glossy icing.

Brown Sugar adds a different flavor and is used in some breads, spice, molasses and fruit cakes. The lighter and finer brown sugar has a more delicate flavor and is recommended where Royal cake recipes call for brown sugar. It may be substituted in equal amounts for granulated sugar.

Maple Sugar and Maple Syrup add a delicate yet distinctive flavor to cakes, icings and fillings. Maple sugar must be grated or shaved, as it ordinarily comes in bars. It is more expensive than either granulated or brown sugar but it may be substituted for them in slightly less quantity.

Molasses, called *golden syrup* or *treacle* in English recipes, is most wholesome and is used in dark fruit, molasses and spice cakes and to flavor breads. It may be substituted for sugar in the same proportion, using a little less liquid. To neutralize the acid, add one-half teaspoon soda for each cup of molasses.

Honey is a wholesome sweet but its flavor is not popular with everyone. It may be used to sweeten breads and may replace all the sweetening in cakes and cookies if ⅓ teaspoon soda is added for each cup honey to neutralize the acid; less liquid is also required.

Eggs

Either brown or white eggs may be used for cakes; the color of the shell does not indicate a different composition but the brown eggs make a deeper yellow cake. Always be sure that they are fresh. Eggs add nutriment, but except when making angel, pound or sponge cake, one egg to each cup of flour is sufficient. When reducing the number of eggs in any recipe add ½ teaspoon Royal Baking Powder for each egg omitted.

Milk

Whole *sweet milk* is intended where recipes call for milk. Soda must be added to *sour milk* or *buttermilk*, ⅓ teaspoonful to one cup of thick sour milk, in addition to the baking powder is the proportion.

Dry or powdered milk may be reliquefied before using, or it may be creamed with the shortening and sugar and the water added as when milk is used. Usually three to four ounces of dry milk are used with a quart of water.

Condensed and evaporated milk may be used in Royal bread and cake recipes. Condensed is sweetened; less sugar should be used with it. Evaporated is unsweetened. Both may be substituted for sweet milk if an equal quantity of water be added.

Flavorings

A cake to be attractive must be delicately and appropriately flavored. Besides vanilla there are many other flavoring extracts: almond, orange, lemon, cinnamon, coffee, anise and rose. Anise is excellent for cookies. Almond and rose are appropriate for angel, pound and white cakes and for frostings and fillings, when used with discretion. Combinations of two flavors are good, for example, lemon and vanilla, or rose and almond.

Lemon juice with grated rind is best for sponge cakes and cookies. Grated orange rind decorates and flavors an icing delicately.

Chocolate and Cocoa

Unsweetened chocolate is meant unless otherwise specified. Chocolate contains more fat than cocoa so that where cocoa is substituted in a cake, use $3\frac{1}{2}$ tablespoons cocoa, and add ½ tablespoon butter for each ounce of chocolate called for.

Either sift cocoa with dry ingredients or mix with just sufficient milk or water to make paste and add directly after egg yolks; two and one-half ounces (or squares) chocolate is generally sufficient for a cake calling for 2 cups of flour, and 1½ ounces chocolate is sufficient for each cup of sugar in icing or filling.

Nuts

Peanuts, hazel nuts, hickory nuts, walnuts, both English and black, and pecans are usually chopped and almonds are chopped or sliced before adding to a batter. Almonds should be blanched before chopping.

Fruits

Raisins (seeded or small seedless), currants, figs, prunes (cooked and raw), dates, citron, angelica (usually for decoration), candied cherries, orange and lemon peel, stewed cranberries, fresh blueberries and even jellies and jams are all good in breads and cakes. Prunes and dates should be pitted before chopping. If fruit is put in oven for a few minutes just before flouring and adding to a cake batter, it will be less likely to sink during the baking. Raisins are plumper and more juicy if heated for three minutes.

All fruit should be well picked over; some must be washed and well drained before flouring with very small amount from the measured flour. Heated and floured scissors will cut fruit without sticking.

How to Open Any Royal Baking Powder Tin

The point to begin cutting the label is indicated by the words—CUT * HERE. Insert the point of knife at the * and cut around entire circumference where cover meets body of tin.

To open, place the tin in the upturned palm of the left hand; put the right hand, palm downward, over the cover, grasping the cover firmly. Give the cover a twist to right and then to left, and it will come off easily.

Should the cover stick, it would indicate that label has not been cut all the way around.

The new Royal tin has an inverted "bead" on the cover about midway between the lower and upper circumference of the cover, that adds materially to the safeguarding of the contents from attacks by moisture.

How to Measure

All measurements must be accurate for success and uniform results every time. Level measurements are intended in all Royal recipes. The standard measuring cup holding one-half pint is intended whenever a cup is mentioned. This cup is marked in thirds and fourths. A set of four cups holding respectively one-fourth, one-third, one-half and one cup, is convenient, newer and also accurate. Do not shake down dry ingredients in cup while they are being measured.

Standard teaspoons and tablespoons singly, or in sets, can be purchased. To measure one cup or one tablespoon or one teaspoon, fill cup or spoon with as much as it will hold and scrape off excess with back of knife. One-half teaspoon or tablespoon is measured level first and then divided lengthwise of spoon; one-third is measured crosswise of spoon.

1 level teaspoon

1 rounding teaspoon

1 heaping teaspoon

In all recipes in this book where one cup, one tablespoon or one teaspoon is called for, the level cup, level tablespoon or level teaspoon is meant.

Table of Measures and Equivalents

1 saltspoon = ¼ teaspoon	16 tablespoons = 1 cup	2 pints = 1 quart
3 teaspoons = 1 tablespoon	2 cups = 1 pint	4 cups = 1 quart

Material	Cups per lb.	Tablespoons per oz.	Material	Cups per lb.	Tablespoons per oz.
Wheat Flour (sifted)	4	4	Raisins	2⅔	1½
Graham "	3¼ approx.	3	Currants	2⅔	1½
Rye "	3½ "	3	Dates	2½	...
Buckwheat "	3 "	3	Prunes	2½	...
Rye Meal	4⅓ "	4	Figs (chopped)	3	...
Rolled Oats	6¼ "	5⅓	Citron (cut)	5½	...
Corn meal	3 "	3	Almonds, chopped	3⅕	2¼
Bran	6¼ "	5⅓	Walnuts (chopped)	3½	2⅔
Rice	2	2	Butter	2	2
Granulated Sugar	2	2	Lard	2	2
Brown "	3 approx.	2¼	Honey	1⅓	1
Powdered "	2½ "	2¾	Salt		2
Confectioners "	3¼ "	3	Royal Baking Powder	2⅓	3
Cornstarch	3	3	Molasses	1⅓	1½
Gelatin		3	Eggs, whole, 10 per pint		
Chocolate (grated)		5½ or 1 sq.	" whites, 18 " "		
Cocoa	3¼ approx.	3½	" yolks, 24 " "		

A Guide to
Proper Temperatures

For Baking

The best and most accurate method of determining oven temperatures is by the use of an automatic oven regulator or a good thermometer placed in the oven before heating. This thermometer should register up to 600° F. or 300° C.

If you have neither, use the "Paper Test". Oven is right temperature when piece of white, unglazed paper placed in center of oven after it is lighted ten minutes colors a light, even brown in the time specified below for each food.

Food	Time	Oven	Degrees Fahr.	Paper Test
White Bread, (baking powder).......	60 minutes	mod.	375°	1 minute
Parker House Rolls—Royal..........	15–20 minutes	hot	425°	¾ minute
Biscuits............................	10–15 minutes	hot	475°	½ minute
Muffins............................	20–25 minutes	mod.-hot	375°–425°	1 minute
Popovers..........................	45 minutes	hot-mod.	*450°–350°	¾ minute
Cup Cakes.........................	20–25 minutes	mod.	†350°–400°	1½ minutes
Layer Cakes.......................	15–20 minutes	mod.	†350°–400°	1½ minutes
Loaf Cakes........................	45–50 minutes	mod.	†325°–375°	2 minutes
Fruit Cakes.......................	3–4 hours	slow	250°	5 minutes
Cookies...........................	10–15 minutes	mod.-hot	†350°–450°	1½ minutes
Angel and Sponge Cakes...........	40–50 minutes	mod.	325°–350°	2 minutes
Custards..........................	60 minutes	slow-mod.	250°–325°	5 minutes
Pastry Shells.....................	10–15 minutes	very hot	500°	½ minute
Pie...............................	30–40 minutes	hot-mod.	†*475°–350°	½ minute
Meringue..........................	15–20 minutes	slow	300°	½ minute

*Reducing temperature last half of baking.
†Depending upon kind of cake, cooky or pie.

To change from Fahrenheit to Centigrade scale, subtract 32° from the degrees Fahrenheit and take ⁵/₉ of that number.

For Deep Fat Frying

If you have no thermometer, use the "Bread Test". Heat the fat slowly until it just begins to smoke, then test by dropping a one-inch cube of bread into the hot fat. Temperature is correct when it browns in the time specified below for each food.

Food	Degrees Fahrenheit	Degrees Centigrade	Bread Test
Fried Chicken.......................	345°–355°	175°–180°	90 seconds
Smelts and Other Fish..............	375°	191°	60 seconds
Doughnuts, Fritters................	375°–385°	191°–196°	60 seconds
Croquettes, Codfish Balls..........	385°	196°	40 seconds
Oysters............................	390°	199°	30 seconds
French Fried Potatoes..............	395°	202°	20 seconds

For Sugar Syrups

If you have no thermometer, use the "Cold Water Test". Test the syrup by dropping a small amount into cold water, until it reaches the stage indicated below. Syrup thermometers may be purchased mounted on a frame which clips onto the side of the saucepan. If an unmounted thermometer is used, hold thermometer in center of the syrup and do not let it touch the bottom or sides of pan.

Food	Degrees Fahrenheit	Degrees Centigrade	Cold Water Test
Fudge Frosting......................	232°	111°	Very Soft Ball
Boiled Frosting....................	238°	114°	Soft Ball
Fudge, Fondant, Penuche............	238°	114°	Soft Ball
Caramels...........................	242°	117°	Firm Ball
Sea Foam Frosting..................	248°	120°	Firm Ball
Glacéd Nuts........................	300°	150°	Brittle

1 Flour should be sifted once before measuring.

2 Measure two cups sifted flour and put in sifter, which has been placed in empty bowl.

5 Measure two tablespoons shortening and put into dry ingredients. If a shorter biscuit is desired, use four tablespoons shortening. Half lard, half butter or other solid fat, can of course be used.

6 Using steel fork, mix shortening lightly and thoroughly with dry ingredients.

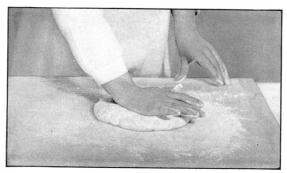

9 Pat dough out lightly with floured hands to about one-half inch thick. If desired, it can be rolled out very lightly with floured rolling pin.

10 Cut out with biscuit cutter dipped in flour. Place on greased pan, far apart if a crusty biscuit is desired, close together if you prefer a thicker and softer biscuit. Gather up pieces of dough and repeat process until all is used.

3 Measure four level teaspoons Royal Baking Powder and one-half teaspoon salt and add to measured flour in the sifter.

4 Sift all dry ingredients; that is, flour, Royal Baking Powder and salt into bowl.

7 Measure three-fourths cup milk and add slowly to dry ingredients just enough to make soft dough. Mix lightly with fork.

8 Toss dough onto slightly floured board.

11 Bake in hot oven at 475° F. about twelve minutes or until nicely browned on top and bottom.

12 Light, flaky hot biscuits ready to serve!

1 FINGER ROLLS—Proceed exactly as for biscuits on page 12, through the mixing of the dough (step 8). Knead lightly with fingers by taking dough farthest away from you and bringing up over towards you.

2 Cut dough with sharp knife into even pieces and shape with floured hands into long smooth rolls. Put into greased roll pan and allow to stand about 20 minutes.

1 PARKER HOUSE ROLLS—Proceed exactly as for biscuits, page 12, through mixing in shortening (step 6); add one egg to one-half cup milk; mix into dough, adding more flour or more milk if necessary; knead lightly until smooth.

2 Roll dough out to about one-third inch thick; cut out with biscuit cutter; crease each with back of knife across center; spread one side with softened butter.

1 ROYAL PHILADELPHIA CINNAMON BUNS —Double the recipe for Parker House Rolls above, rolling dough very thin. Spread with softened butter; sprinkle with brown sugar, cinnamon and raisins.

2 Beginning at edge nearest you roll dough up carefully as you do for a jelly roll.

3 CLOVERLEAF ROLLS—Cut dough into smaller pieces, rolling into little balls and putting three in each greased muffin tin and allow to stand about 20 minutes.

4 Brushed with milk or butter and then baked in hot oven at 425° F. for 15 minutes and served hot they are delicious for luncheon or supper.

3 Fold one side well over other and allow to stand about 20 minutes in greased pan.

4 Baked in hot oven at 425° F. for 20 minutes, they make a delicious change for either breakfast, luncheon or supper.

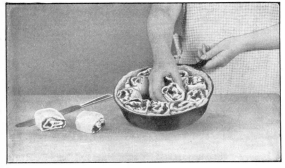

3 Cream six tablespoons butter with six tablespoons brown sugar; spread thickly on bottom and sides of iron skillet or baking pan; with sharp knife cut dough into two-inch pieces and place with cut edges up in pan.

4 After standing about 20 minutes, these buns are baked in hot oven at 425° F. for 25 minutes and are removed from pan at once turning upside down to serve.

THE ROYAL MASTER RECIPE FOR
BAKING POWDER BISCUITS

2 cups flour
4 teaspoons Royal Baking Powder
½ teaspoon salt
2 tablespoons shortening
¾ cup milk or half milk and half
  water

Makes fourteen biscuits.

Sift together flour, baking powder and salt; add shortening and mix in thoroughly with steel fork. Add liquid slowly to make soft dough. Roll or pat out with hands on floured board to about one-half inch in thickness. Cut with biscuit cutter, first dipped in flour. Place on slightly greased pan and bake in hot oven at 475° F. ten to twelve minutes. If a shorter biscuit is desired, use three or four tablespoons shortening.

Royal Biscuits can be baked immediately after mixing or they can be covered and set aside in a cool place for baking several hours later or even the next day. If kept in ice box allow to stand in kitchen a few minutes before baking.

Because two acid reacting ingredients, cream of tartar and tartaric acid, are combined in Royal, the dough begins to rise as soon as mixed and continues to rise when put into the oven or when heat is applied. This is what is meant by "double acting."

DELICIOUS VARIATIONS OF THE MASTER RECIPE

Whole Wheat or Graham Biscuit

Take one cup whole wheat or graham flour and one cup white flour, one tablespoon granulated or brown sugar and proceed exactly as in the Master Recipe, baking about fourteen minutes. All whole wheat or graham flour can be used if desired.

Makes fourteen biscuits.

Cheese Biscuit

Omit shortening in Master Recipe and add eight tablespoons grated cheese, blending with flour.

Makes sixteen biscuits.

Bran Biscuit

Follow recipe for Golden Tea Biscuit, using one and one-quarter cups flour and three-fourths cup bran. Roll to one-third inch thick and bake about fifteen minutes.

Makes fourteen biscuits.

Fruit Biscuit

Make as for whole wheat biscuit, adding one more tablespoon sugar and one-half cup chopped dates or seeded raisins to dry ingredients.

Makes fourteen biscuits.

Virginia Biscuit

Add one tablespoon sugar to dry ingredients in Master Recipe and replace all shortening with peanut butter, mixing in the peanut butter exactly as you would plain shortening.

Makes fourteen biscuits.

Lightning Biscuit

Follow Master Recipe, using one-quarter cup more milk to make a softer dough. Drop by spoonfuls on greased baking sheet or in muffin tins and bake immediately.

Makes fifteen biscuits.

Nut Biscuit

Make as for whole wheat biscuit, adding one more tablespoon sugar, one-half cup chopped pecan or walnut meats to dry ingredients and put a pinch of chopped nuts on top of each before baking.

Makes fourteen biscuits.

Golden Tea Biscuit

Follow Master Recipe, using three teaspoons Royal Baking Powder instead of four, and adding one tablespoon sugar to the dry ingredients. Mix one egg with one-half cup water and use for liquid instead of milk.

Makes fourteen biscuits.

Butter Cakes or "Ovenless Bread"

Follow Master Recipe, rolling dough to one-fourth inch thick. Place biscuits on slightly greased and hot griddle or iron frying pan and bake on top of stove until well browned and puffed up; turn and brown other side. Split and butter liberally and send piping hot to table.

Makes fourteen butter cakes.

Individual Chicken Shortcakes

2 cups flour	4 tablespoons shortening
3 teaspoons Royal Baking Powder	1 egg
½ teaspoon salt	½ cup water

Sift together flour, baking powder and salt. Add shortening and mix in thoroughly with steel fork. Add egg and sufficient water to make soft dough. Cut with any large biscuit cutter which has been dipped in flour, or half fill greased muffin rings which have been placed on baking pan and bake in hot oven at 475° F. ten to twelve minutes.

These shortcakes split and either buttered or not, as desired, filled with hot creamed chicken or mushrooms make a delicious dish.

If one tablespoon sugar is sifted with the dry ingredients, these shortcakes can also be used with any fruit desired.

Makes six shortcakes.

Orange Biscuit

2 cups flour	4 teaspoons Royal Baking Powder
1 tablespoon sugar	3 tablespoons shortening
½ teaspoon salt	¾ cup milk

Sift dry ingredients; add shortening and mix in with fork Add liquid slowly to make soft dough. Turn out on floured board; roll or pat to one-half inch thick. Cut out with small biscuit cutter and put on greased pan. Press gently into center of each biscuit a loaf of sugar which has been dipped well in orange juice. Grate a little orange rind on each and bake in hot oven at 475° F. about fifteen minutes.

Makes fifteen biscuits.

Brown or Maple Sugar Biscuit

2 cups flour	4 tablespoons shortening
½ teaspoon salt	¾ cup milk
4 teaspoons Royal Baking Powder	brown or maple sugar

Sift dry ingredients into bowl; mix in shortening; add milk to make soft dough. Pat or roll out to one-half inch thick; cut with small biscuit cutter. Spread with softened butter and thickly with brown or grated maple sugar and a little cinnamon, if desired. Bake in greased pan in moderate oven at 400° F. for fifteen minutes.

Makes sixteen biscuits.

Sandwich or Picnic Biscuit

2 cups flour	2 tablespoons shortening
4 teaspoons Royal Baking Powder	¾ cup milk
½ teaspoon salt	

Sift together flour, baking powder and salt. Add shortening and mix in thoroughly with steel fork. Add liquid slowly to make soft dough. Roll dough to one-fourth inch thick; cut with small biscuit cutter. Spread half rounds with creamed butter and thickly with chopped ham or other meat; cover with remaining rounds; press together and brush tops and sides with milk. Bake in greased pan in hot oven at 475° F. for ten to twelve minutes.

Makes fourteen sandwiches.

Scones

2 cups flour	2 tablespoons sugar
3 teaspoons Royal Baking Powder	3 tablespoons shortening
1 teaspoon salt	2 eggs
	⅛ cup milk

Sift dry ingredients; add shortening and mix in lightly. Beat eggs; add milk to eggs and add to mixture. Roll or pat out to one-half inch thick on floured board; shape into three large rounds, cut each round at right angles into four parts, making them three-cornered; brush with milk; sprinkle with sugar. Bake in greased pan in moderate oven at 400° F. about twenty-five minutes.

For fruit scones add 1 cup raisins or currants before the liquid.

Makes twelve scones.

Rye Rolls

1 cup flour	6 teaspoons Royal Baking Powder
3 cups rye flour	1 ½ cups milk
1 teaspoon salt	1 tablespoon melted shortening

Sift dry ingredients together; add melted shortening and milk to make soft dough. Knead on floured board; shape into rolls. Put into greased pans and allow to stand in warm place twenty minutes. Bake in hot oven at 475° F. fifteen to twenty minutes.

Makes twelve rolls.

Boston Brown Bread

1 cup whole wheat or graham flour	5 teaspoons Royal Baking Powder
	1 teaspoon salt
1 cup corn meal	¾ cup dark molasses
1 cup rye meal or ground rolled oats	1⅛ cups milk

Mix dry ingredients thoroughly; add molasses to milk, and add to dry ingredients; beat thoroughly and put into greased moulds two-thirds full. Cover tightly and steam three and one-half hours; remove covers and bake in moderate oven at 400° F. until top is dry.

Makes one large or three small loaves.

Individual Chicken Pie
Pastry

1 cup flour	½ teaspoon salt
2 teaspoons Royal Baking Powder	4 tablespoons shortening
	cold water

Sift dry ingredients and rub in shortening; add just enough water to make stiff dough. Roll out thin and cover pie which has been put in individual baking dish. Trim off paste and bake in very hot oven at 500° F. for five to six minutes.

For each pie cook three or four small onions, about five small young carrots, a few fresh peas, one potato cut into small pieces and two or three slices of breast of chicken. Put in a rather thin, nicely seasoned gravy or cream sauce. Creamed mushrooms, left-over lamb, cut into small pieces and covered with gravy with this pie crust make excellent variations.

Pastry is sufficient to cover three pies.

Royal Individual Coffee Cakes

2 cups flour	4 tablespoons shortening
¾ teaspoon salt	1 egg
4 tablespoons sugar	½ cup milk
3 teaspoons Royal Baking Powder	

Sift dry ingredients together; mix in shortening; add beaten egg to milk and add to dry ingredients to make soft dough; divide dough into six long, narrow pieces; with hands roll each piece on board until long and thin; spread with butter; cut each in two and beginning in center twist two pieces together and bring ends around to form crescent. Put into greased pan; sprinkle with chopped nuts. Bake in hot oven at 450° F. fifteen to twenty minutes. While hot, brush over with thin icing made with one-half cup confectioner's sugar moistened with one tablespoon hot water.

Makes six coffee cakes.

Quick Coffee Cake

2 cups flour	4 teaspoons Royal Baking Powder
½ teaspoon salt	2 tablespoons shortening, melted
3 tablespoons sugar	1 cup milk

Sift dry ingredients into bowl; add melted shortening and enough milk to make very stiff batter. Mix well and spread one-half inch thick in greased pan; add top mixture. Bake about thirty minutes in moderate oven at 400° F.

Top Mixture

3 tablespoons flour	3 tablespoons sugar
1 tablespoon cinnamon	3 tablespoons shortening

Mix dry ingredients; rub in shortening and spread thickly over top of dough before baking.

Makes one nine-inch coffee cake.

Fruit Bread

1 cup prunes, figs or dates	1 teaspoon salt
2 ½ cups graham flour or 1 cup flour and 1 ½ cups graham flour	5 teaspoons Royal Baking Powder
	1 cup milk
¼ cup sugar	1 tablespoon shortening, melted

Stone and chop fruit (prunes can be soaked several hours and drained or used right after washing thoroughly). Mix graham flour with the wheat flour, sugar, salt and baking powder which have been sifted together; add milk to make soft dough and beat well; add fruit and shortening. Put into greased bread pan; allow to stand twenty to twenty-five minutes in warm place. Bake in moderate oven at 375° F. one hour.

Makes one large loaf.

Corn Bread

1 cup corn meal	½ teaspoon salt
1 cup flour	1 egg
4 teaspoons Royal Baking Powder	1 ½ cups milk
1 tablespoon sugar	4 tablespoons shortening, melted

Sift together corn meal, flour, baking powder, sugar and salt. Add beaten egg and milk to make a stiff batter. Add shortening and beat until light and thoroughly mixed. Pour into greased shallow pan. Bake in hot oven at 425° F. about twenty-five minutes.

Makes one sheet eight inches square.

Royal Philadelphia Cinnamon Buns

3 cups flour	1 egg
2 tablespoons sugar	⅔ cup water
1 teaspoon salt	½ cup brown sugar
6 teaspoons Royal Baking Powder	2 teaspoons cinnamon
2 tablespoons shortening	6 tablespoons raisins

Sift two tablespoons sugar with flour, salt and baking powder; rub shortening in lightly; add beaten egg to water and add slowly. Roll out one-fourth inch thick on floured bread; brush with softened butter; sprinkle thickly with brown sugar, cinnamon and raisins. Roll as for jelly roll. Have prepared six tablespoons butter creamed with six tablespoons brown sugar. Spread this mixture on bottom and sides of iron baking pan, or if this cannot be obtained an iron skillet will do. Cut dough into one and one-half inch pieces and place with cut edges up on pan. Allow to stand about fifteen minutes and bake in hot oven at 425° F. twenty-five minutes. Remove from pan at once, turning upside down to serve.

Makes eight large buns.

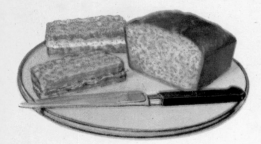

Peanut Butter Bread

2 cups flour	⅓ cup sugar
4 teaspoons Royal Baking Powder	½ cup peanut butter
1 teaspoon salt	1½ cups milk

Sift flour, Royal Baking Powder, salt and sugar together into bowl; add peanut butter and mix in as for biscuits. Add milk and beat thoroughly; put into one large or two small greased oblong loaf pans; smooth tops before baking and bake in moderate oven at 350° F. about one hour.

Makes two small or one large loaf.

Cheese Straws

1 cup grated American cheese	¹⁄₁₆ teaspoon cayenne pepper
1 cup flour	¼ teaspoon paprika
1 teaspoon Royal Baking Powder	1 egg
½ teaspoon salt	2 tablespoons milk

Mix together cheese, flour, baking powder, salt, cayenne pepper and paprika; add beaten egg; mix well; add milk enough to make a stiff dough. Roll out one-eighth inch thick, on floured board; cut into strips five inches long and one-fourth inch wide. Bake in hot oven at 450° F. ten minutes.

Makes thirty Cheese Straws.

Nut and Raisin Rolls

2½ cups flour	⅔ cup milk
4 teaspoons Royal Baking Powder	butter
½ teaspoon salt	raisins
1 tablespoon sugar	chopped nuts
5 tablespoons shortening, melted	sugar
1 egg	egg yolk

Sift first four ingredients together. Add shortening, and beaten egg to milk and add to dry ingredients, mixing well. Turn out on floured board and knead lightly. Roll out very thin. Spread with softened butter and sprinkle with raisins, chopped nuts and small amount of granulated sugar. Cut into about four-inch squares. Roll up each as for jelly roll. Press edges together, brush over with yolk of egg mixed with a little cold water and sprinkle with nuts and sugar, and allow to stand in greased pan about fifteen minutes. Bake in moderate oven at 400° F. from twenty to twenty-five minutes.

Makes eighteen rolls.

Luncheon Rolls

4 cups flour	1 tablespoon shortening
1 teaspoon salt	1½ cups milk
6 teaspoons Royal Baking Powder	

Sift dry ingredients; rub in shortening; add milk, and mix to smooth dough easy to handle on floured board. Knead dough quickly a few times to impart smoothness; divide into small pieces; form each by hand into short, rather thick tapering roll; place on greased pans and allow to stand in warm place fifteen minutes; brush with milk. Bake in hot oven at 450° F. about twenty minutes. When almost baked brush with melted butter. Bake ten minutes longer and serve hot. If a glazed finish is desired, before taking from oven brush with yolk of egg which has been mixed with a little water. These rolls make excellent sandwiches, using for fillings, either lettuce and mayonnaise, sliced or chopped ham, chopped seasoned cucumbers or egg and mayonnaise with very little chopped onion and parsley.

Makes twelve rolls.

THICK sour milk, sour cream and buttermilk (that is sour), can each be used in place of sweet milk if these instructions are carefully followed. Use one-third teaspoon soda to each cup of thick sour milk and add Royal Baking Powder as directed in the recipe for sweet milk.

Beeause sour cream contains so much fat, the butter or other shortening in the recipe will have to be reduced when sour cream is used.

Soda can be sifted with the dry ingredients or added to the sour milk. Either method is satisfactory with perhaps a little advantage in the former.

Where other acid-reacting materials such as molasses, raisins, bran and brown sugar are also included in a sour milk recipe, the amount of soda will, of course, have to be increased slightly.

Emergency or Sour Milk Biscuits

2 cups flour	¼ teaspoon soda
4 teaspoons Royal Baking Powder	4 tablespoons shortening
½ teaspoon salt	¾ cup sour milk

Sift flour, baking powder, salt and soda together. Melt shortening, add to sour milk and add this liquid to the dry ingredients. Mix to make a soft dough. Turn out on slightly floured board. Roll or pat out to one-half inch thick. Cut with small biscuit cutter and place on slightly greased pan. Bake in hot oven at 475° F. for twelve minutes.
Buttermilk can be used instead of sour milk.
Makes sixteen biscuits.

Sour Milk Waffles

1 egg	1 teaspoon Royal Baking Powder
1½ cups sour milk or buttermilk	½ teaspoon salt
1½ cups flour	2 tablespoons melted butter
1 teaspoon soda	

Beat egg until very light. Add milk and flour sifted with soda, baking powder and salt. Then add melted butter. Beat well and bake in hot greased waffle iron until golden brown. If electric iron is used no grease will be necessary.
Sour cream may be used instead of sour milk or buttermilk. When it is used omit the butter.
Makes five large waffles.

Sour Milk Bran Muffins

1 cup flour	1 egg
3 teaspoons Royal Baking Powder	4 tablespoons shortening, melted
¼ teaspoon salt	1 cup sour milk
½ teaspoon soda	2 tablespoons molasses
2 tablespoons sugar	½ cup seeded and floured raisins
1¾ cups bran	

Sift together flour, baking powder, salt, soda and sugar. Add bran. Beat egg, add shortening and milk. Add to dry ingredients. Add molasses. Stir in raisins. Bake in greased muffin tins in moderate oven at 400° F. for twenty to twenty-five minutes.
Makes ten muffins.

Sour Milk Griddle Cakes

1½ cups flour	⅓ teaspoon soda
½ teaspoon salt	1 egg
2 teaspoons Royal Baking Powder	1½ cups sour milk
	2 tablespoons shortening

Sift dry ingredients together; add egg, milk and shortening which has been melted. Mix well and bake by spoonfuls on hot, very slightly greased griddle. Turn once only and serve immediately.
Makes twenty cakes.

Sour Milk Corn Meal Muffins

1 cup corn meal	2 tablespoons sugar
¾ cup flour	1 egg
3 teaspoons Royal Baking Powder	1 cup sour milk
¼ teaspoon soda	4 tablespoons melted butter
½ teaspoon salt	

Sift dry ingredients together. Add egg, milk and melted butter. Bake in greased muffin tins in moderate oven starting at 350° F. and increasing to 385° F. Bake for twenty minutes.
Makes twelve muffins.

James River Waffles
Reprinted through courtesy of
"Good Housekeeping" and adapted to use Royal

3 eggs	¼ teaspoon salt
2 cups thick sour milk	1 teaspoon soda
2 cups flour	6 tablespoons butter, melted
2 teaspoons Royal Baking Powder	

Separate eggs. Beat yolks, add one cup sour milk. Sift dry ingredients; add to yolks. Add other cup sour milk; add butter and stiffly beaten egg whites. Bake in hot greased waffle iron unless electric iron is used, then no grease is necessary. Serve with butter and hot maple syrup.
Makes eight waffles.

Raisin Spice Cake

¼ cup shortening	3 teaspoons Royal Baking Powder
1 cup sugar	
1 egg	⅓ teaspoon soda
1 teaspoon vanilla extract	½ teaspoon salt
2 cups flour	1 cup sour milk
1½ teaspoons cinnamon	1 cup seedless raisins, floured
1 teaspoon nutmeg	

Cream shortening; add sugar slowly; add well beaten egg and flavoring; sift together flour, spices, baking powder, soda and salt; add to mixture, a little at a time, alternately with milk; add floured raisins which have been heated. Bake in greased loaf pan in moderate oven at 350° F. about fifty minutes.
Makes one small loaf.

Mocha Cream Cup Cakes

¼ teaspoon soda	¼ cup strong coffee
4 tablespoons heavy sour cream	1½ cups flour
1 cup light brown sugar	½ teaspoon salt
1 egg	3 teaspoons Royal Baking Powder
¼ cup milk	1 teaspoon vanilla extract

Add soda to cream and mix. Blend thoroughly with sugar. Add egg yolk and beat well. Mix milk and coffee and add. Add flour sifted with baking powder and salt. Mix well. Add vanilla, beaten egg white and bake in greased small tins in moderate oven at 400° F. about twenty minutes.
Makes twenty small cakes.

1 QUICK GRAHAM BREAD—Sift one and one-half cups sifted flour, four teaspoons Royal Baking Powder, one and one-fourth teaspoons salt, two tablespoons sugar together into bowl.

2 Add one and one-half cups graham flour, one tablespoon melted shortening, two cups milk, or just enough to make a soft dough and beat thoroughly until smooth.

1 PEANUT BUTTER BREAD—Sift two cups sifted flour, four teaspoons Royal Baking Powder, one teaspoon salt, one-third cup sugar into bowl.

2 Add one-half cup peanut butter and mix in well. Add one and one-half cups milk, mixing to soft dough.

1 NUT AND RAISIN BREAD—Sift one and one-half cups sifted flour, five teaspoons Royal Baking Powder, one teaspoon salt, one-third teaspoon soda into bowl. Mix in one and one-half cups graham flour, one cup seeded raisins, three-fourths cup chopped nuts.

2 Mix one-fourth cup dark molasses and one-half cup brown sugar with one and one-half cups milk. Mix thoroughly and add to dry ingredients.

3 Put into greased loaf pan and smooth top with melted shortening.

4 The loaf is baked in moderate oven at 375° F. about one hour and is then turned upside down to cool before the pan is removed. This makes the crust softer and easier to slice.

3 Beat thoroughly and put in greased loaf pan; smooth top and bake in moderate oven at 350° F. about one hour.

4 Cooled in pan and the next day made into delicious sandwiches!

3 Grease two 12-ounce Royal tins or two very small oblong pans; fill three-fourths full. Smooth tops and bake in moderate oven at 375° F. about one hour.

4 This bread is cooled in pans and then sliced. It is excellent either plain or for sandwiches. Dates can be used instead of raisins and make a delicious and wholesome loaf.

1 Measure two cups sifted flour and three teaspoons Royal Baking Powder into sifter placed in bowl.

2 Measure one-half teaspoon salt and one tablespoon sugar into other dry ingredients.

5 Add one cup milk a little at a time to make a rather stiff batter and with a light motion beat well until smooth.

6 Add four tablespoons butter or other shortening which has been melted and cooled. It saves time to melt the butter in the muffin tins or in tin cup held over hot water or low flame.

9 Bake in moderate oven at 400° F. 18 to 20 minutes.

10 Always serve muffins hot in a napkin on hot plate and immediately after taking from the oven.

3 Sift all dry ingredients together into bowl.

4 Break two eggs into dry ingredients.

7 Mix well by stirring and do not beat. The batter is just soft enough to pour as shown in next picture.

8 Half fill greased muffin tins.

11 Muffins are excellent served with butter and maple syrup—or with honey.

12 Keep any left-over muffins and split, toast and butter them for luncheon, tea or supper.

THE menus suggested on the page following are all arranged with proper balance of foods in mind and without neglecting appropriateness and attractiveness of combinations.

For convenience and as a reminder, to give variety to your meals and not to neglect the more uncommon foods, all or practically all are listed in groups below.

A minimum of one cooked and one raw green vegetable should be included in each day's menu.

Similar vegetables such as macaroni and white potatoes or macaroni and rice or potatoes and rice should not be served at the same meal.

Color contrasts should be considered in arranging all meals.

There are certain combinations of foods to which we have become accustomed that are happily dietetically correct; for example, corned beef and cabbage, pig's knuckles and sauerkraut, roast duck or goose and apples, roast pork and apple sauce, roast veal and tomatoes, buckwheat cakes and sausage, fish and cucumbers. It is always necessary to plan ahead so that meats and vegetables left over from one meal will not be served in exactly the same way at the meal following. Left-over spinach may well appear as creamed spinach au gratin or left-over lamb as lamb with piquante sauce. One or two tomatoes, sweet potatoes, pieces of eggplant and asparagus left over from one meal may be broiled the next day for a most attractive broiled vegetable luncheon.

All the foods listed below are not available in every locality, but sufficient choice is possible to give every week's menus some variety. Creamed soups can be made from practically every vegetable listed and most of the vegetables can be prepared in a great variety of ways.

FOODS FROM WHICH TO CHOOSE

VEGETABLES	FRUITS	MEAT—Cont.	FISH
Peas	Oranges	Beef, dried	Bass
String beans	Lemons	heart	Cod, fresh
Lima Beans	Limes	tongue	salt
Butter beans	Kumquats	Calves' head	Bluefish
Kidney beans	Grapefruit	brains	Shad
Lentils	Grapes	liver	roe
Spinach	Plums	Oxtail	Carp
Asparagus	Prunes	Sweetbreads	Finnan haddie
Green peppers	Apricots	Tripe	Flounder
Brussels sprouts	Peaches	Veal, cutlet	Pike
Broccoli	Pears	loin	Pickerel
Artichokes	Quinces	shoulder	Trout
Jerusalem artichokes	Watermelon	chops	Salmon
Zuccini	Cantaloupe	Lamb and Mutton, leg	Eels
Okra	Persian melon	shoulder	Weakfish
Kohlrabi	Casaba melon	loin chops	Halibut
Beet greens	Honeydew melon	rib chops	Mackerel
Dandelion greens	Guava	steaks	Haddock
Chard	Mangoes	kidneys	Herring, fresh
Cauliflower	Avocado	Pork, loin	smoked
Oyster plant	Bananas	chops	salt
Egg plant	Figs	tenderloin	Swordfish
Onions	Apples	fresh ham	Sturgeon
Leeks	Pineapple	smoked ham	Sardines
Beets	Rhubarb	salt	Whitebait
Cucumbers	Pomegranate	bacon	Tuna
Tomatoes	Persimmons	sausages	Turbot
Squash	Nectarines	scrapple	Sole
Carrots	Cherries	pig's feet	Whitefish
Turnips	Cranberries	head cheese	Smelts
Pumpkin	Strawberries	suckling pig	Butterfish
Celery	Blueberries	Turkey	Perch
Corn	Huckleberries	Chicken	Pompano
Sweet potatoes	Blackberries	Fowl	Turtle
White potatoes	Loganberries	Capon	Frog's legs
Yams	Raspberries	Guinea hen	Terrapin
Rice	Gooseberries	Duck	Lobster
Wild rice	Currants	Wild duck	Crawfish
Hominy	Raisins	Goose	Crabs
Macaroni	Olives	Pigeon	Clams
Mushrooms		Squab	Oysters
Lettuce		Quail	Scallops
Field lettuce	**MEAT**	Partridge	Shrimp
Cal. lettuce		Rabbit	Mussels
Chicory	Beef, ribs	Venison	Snails
Endive	round		
Romaine	steak		
Watercress	corned		
Radishes	filet		
	chopped		

SOME SIMPLE BREAKFASTS, LUNCHEONS AND DINNERS

WARM WEATHER BREAKFASTS

FRUIT	CEREAL	MAIN DISH	BREAD
Strawberries and Cream	Trisket	Broiled Smoked Salmon	Popovers
Pineapple Juice	Toasties	Poached Eggs	Blueberry Muffins
Honey Dew Melon	Pettijohns	Fried Smelts	Parker House Rolls
Grape Fruit Juice	Shredded Wheat	Broiled Ham	Bran Muffins
Raspberries and Cream	Cream of Wheat	Parsley Scrambled Eggs	Royal Coffee Cake
Halved Peaches	Corn Flakes	Creamed Tuna Fish	Hot Biscuits with Marmalade

With Milk, Coffee, Cocoa or Tea

COLD WEATHER BREAKFASTS

Grapes	Hominy	Codfish Balls	Cinnamon Buns
Orange Juice	Oatmeal	Kippered Herring	Poppy Muffins
Stewed Figs	Mush	Sausages	Buckwheat Cakes
Stewed Prunes	Pettijohns	Creamed Codfish	Rice Griddle Cakes
Orange Juice	Rolled Oats	Kidney Stew	Crisp Corn Bread
Apricots	Shredded Wheat	Spanish Omelet	Scones

With Milk, Coffee, Cocoa or Tea

WARM WEATHER LUNCHEONS

MAIN DISH	VEGETABLES	BREAD	SALAD	DESSERT
Broiled Fresh Vegetables		Corn Bread		Fruit Ice Cream, Sand Tarts
Lobster Newburg	Spinach	Toast Melba	Jellied Cucumber	
Fried Soft Shell Crabs	Potatoes au gratin	Sally Lunn		Fresh Raspberry Tarts
Hamburg Steak	Cold Tomatoes and Hot Okra	Cheese Biscuits		Chocolate Layer Cake and Pineapple
Chicken Shortcake	Fresh Peas	Bran Biscuits		Lemon Jelly

With Iced Tea, Coffee, Chocolate, Milk or Gingerale

COLD WEATHER LUNCHEONS

Oyster and Mushroom Poulette	Saratoga Chips	Hot Rolls	Pears and Cream Cheese	Pumpkin Pie
Spinach and Egg Salad		Corn Muffins		Caramel Custard, Cup Cakes, Chocolate Icing
Beefsteak Pie	String Beans	Nut and Fruit Bread	Tomato Jelly	Orange Cream Meringue
Stuffed Peppers	Macaroni and Cheese	Pecan Muffins		Compote of Fruit
Rice Croquettes	Carrots and Peas	Luncheon Rolls	Escarole Vinaigrette	Cottage Pudding, Foamy Sauce

With Tea, Coffee, Milk or Chocolate

WARM WEATHER DINNERS

FIRST COURSE	MAIN DISH	VEGETABLES	SALAD	DESSERT
Lobster Cocktail	Broiled Chicken	Peas, New Potatoes	Romaine and Cream Cheese	
Hors-d'oeuvres	Filet Mignon	Broccoli Hollandaise, Potatoes au gratin		Pineapple Sherbet
Jellied Bouillon	Baked Fish	String Beans, French Fried Potatoes	Endive	Peach Shortcake
Lamb Broth	Broiled Fish	Baked Tomatoes, Potato Puffs	Cucumber	Berry Pie
Cream of Spinach Soup	Lamb Chops	Summer Squash, Lima Beans	Lettuce, Paprika Dressing	Strawberry Mousse
Clams on Half Shell	Roast Duck, Apple Rings	Riced Potatoes, Asparagus	Celery, Mayonnaise	Peach Sherbet, Wafers

Serve Dinner Rolls, Toast Melba or Bread with above and a Demi-Tasse after.

COLD WEATHER DINNERS

Oysters on Half Shell	Stuffed Roast Veal	Spinach, Sweet Potatoes	Waldorf, Mayonnaise	Pineapple Bavarian Cream
Purée Mongole	Roast Lamb, Mint Jelly	Wild Rice, Broccoli	Green Pepper and Cheese	Fig Pudding
Cream of Celery	Loin of Pork, Apple Sauce	Cauliflower, Buttered Beets	Endive	Prune Soufflé
Shrimp Cocktail	Roast Guinea Hen	Creamed Oyster Plant, String Beans	White Grape	Vanilla Ice Cream, Chocolate Sauce
Assorted Hors-d'oeuvres	Broiled Steak	Creamed Onions, Baked Egg Plant	Watercress, French Dressing	Deep Apple Pie
Chicken Soup	Corned Beef	Brussels Sprouts, Stuffed Potatoes	Cold Slaw	Apple Dumplings, Hard Sauce

Serve Dinner Rolls, Finger Rolls, Toast Melba or Bread with above and a Demi-Tasse after.

THE ROYAL MASTER RECIPE FOR MUFFINS

2 cups flour
3 teaspoons Royal Baking Powder
1 tablespoon sugar
½ teaspoon salt
2 eggs
1 cup milk
4 tablespoons melted shortening

Makes fourteen muffins.

Sift together flour, baking powder, sugar and salt; add eggs, milk, melted and cooled shortening to make a stiff batter; mix all together well. Half fill greased muffin tins and bake in moderate oven at 400° F. eighteen to twenty minutes.

TEN DELICIOUS VARIATIONS OF THE MASTER RECIPE

Bran Muffins

Follow Master Recipe using equal parts white flour, bran and graham flour instead of flour indicated. Add one more teaspoon Royal Baking Powder and three tablespoons brown sugar or dark molasses. Omit one egg.

Makes twelve muffins.

Corn Meal Muffins

Follow Master Recipe, using three-fourths cup corn meal and one and one-quarter cups flour instead of all flour; add one tablespoon more sugar (or omit all sugar) and use one egg instead of two.

Makes twelve muffins.

Crumb Muffins

Take two cups stale bread crumbs and one cup flour instead of two; add crumbs to other dry ingredients and follow Master Recipe.

Makes twelve muffins.

Ginger Muffins

Sift one-fourth teaspoon soda, one-half teaspoon ginger with dry ingredients in Master Recipe; use one-half cup molasses and one-half cup milk instead of one cup milk; one egg instead of two; and two more tablespoons shortening, and bake in moderate oven at 375° F. Serve hot with butter.

Makes sixteen muffins.

Cocoanut Muffins

Follow Master Recipe, using one egg instead of two; omit shortening and add one-half cup shredded cocoanut. Bake in small greased muffin tins.

Makes twenty-four small muffins.

Date or Fruit Muffins

Follow Master Recipe, using one egg instead of two and little less milk. Flour two-thirds cup chopped and pitted dates or seedless raisins and add to batter.

For a sweet fruit muffin add one-fourth cup more sugar.

For a delightful variety use one-half cup finely chopped candied cherries and citron instead of above fruit.

Makes twelve muffins.

Poppy Muffins

To the muffin batter of Master Recipe add two teaspoons poppy seeds and bake as directed.

Makes fourteen muffins.

Graham Gems

Follow directions for Master Recipe, using one cup graham flour and one cup white flour; one egg instead of two; four teaspoons Royal Baking Powder instead of three; and two tablespoons sugar instead of one.

Makes twelve gems.

Raspberry Dainties

Stir four tablespoons raspberry jam into muffin batter of Master Recipe.

Strawberry or other jam may be used.

Makes fourteen muffins.

Chocolate Muffins

Add two more tablespoons sugar to Master Recipe and stir one and one-half squares (1½ oz.) grated unsweetened chocolate in batter just before putting in tins.

Makes fourteen muffins.

Cereal Muffins

½ cup cooked hominy, oatmeal, rice or other cereal	½ cup milk
½ teaspoon salt	1½ cups flour
2 tablespoons shortening	2 tablespoons sugar
1 egg	4 teaspoons Royal Baking Powder

Mix together cereal, salt, shortening which has been melted, beaten egg and milk. Add flour and sugar which have been sifted with baking powder; beat well. Bake in greased muffin tins in moderate oven at 400° F. twenty-five to thirty minutes.

Makes fourteen muffins.

Waffles

2 cups flour	2 eggs
½ teaspoon salt	1¾ cups milk
3 teaspoons Royal Baking Powder	4 tablespoons shortening

Sift all dry ingredients into bowl; add yolks of eggs and milk. Beat well and add shortening which has been melted and cooled. Beat egg whites until stiff and fold into batter; mix, but do not beat. Pour three or four tablespoons of batter into the center of very hot, well-greased waffle iron (if electric iron is used no grease is necessary); spread batter slightly; close iron and bake about 1¼ minutes or until well puffed up and brown on one side; turn and bake about three-fourths of a minute. Remove at once to hot plate and serve immediately with plenty of butter and maple syrup. For a richer waffle use ½ cup shortening, half butter and half lard.

The secret of good waffles is a hot waffle iron, which should be kept at an even temperature throughout baking.

Makes eighteen servings or four and one-half waffles.

Chocolate Waffles

½ cup butter	1 teaspoon Royal Baking Powder
¾ cup sugar	
2 eggs	6 tablespoons cocoa
1 teaspoon vanilla extract	½ teaspoon cinnamon
1¼ cups flour	½ teaspoon salt

Cream butter and add sugar slowly.

Add beaten eggs, flavoring and all the dry ingredients, sifted together. Heat waffle iron about five minutes. (It must not be as hot as for regular waffles). Grease iron very slightly. If electric iron is used no greasing is necessary. Put three or four tablespoons of batter into center of the iron. Spread batter slightly. Bake about two or three minutes. Serve warm with ice cream or slightly sweetened whipped cream.

Makes four to five waffles.

Buckwheat Cakes

1 cup buckwheat flour	1¼ cups milk or milk and water
½ cup flour	
3 teaspoons Royal Baking Powder	2 teaspoons molasses
¾ teaspoon salt	1 tablespoon melted shortening

Sift together flours, baking powder and salt; add molasses and shortening to liquid; combine ingredients and beat well. Bake on hot slightly greased griddle turning only once.

Makes twelve cakes.

Royal Griddle Cakes

2 cups flour	1½ cups milk
½ teaspoon salt	2 tablespoons melted shortening
4 teaspoons Royal Baking Powder	
2 eggs	

Sift dry ingredients into bowl; add beaten eggs, milk and melted shortening. Mix well and bake by spoonfuls on slightly greased hot griddle. When bubbles appear turn cakes and brown other side. Do not turn a second time. Serve immediately on hot plate with butter and maple syrup.

Excellent Royal Griddle Cakes can be made omitting the eggs and using 5 teaspoons Royal Baking Powder.

Makes twelve cakes.

Rice Griddle Cakes

1 cup boiled rice	1 teaspoon salt
1 cup milk	1 egg
1 tablespoon melted shortening	1 cup flour
2 teaspoons Royal Baking Powder	

Mix rice, milk, melted shortening, salt and well-beaten egg; stir in flour and baking powder which have been sifted together; mix well. Bake on hot, slightly greased griddle turning only once.

Makes twelve small cakes.

Popovers

1 cup flour	1 tablespoon shortening
¼ teaspoon salt	1 cup milk
2 eggs	

Sift together flour and salt. Make a well in flour, break eggs into well, add melted shortening and milk and stir until smooth. Pour into hot greased gem pans and put into hot oven, at 450° F. for thirty minutes; decrease heat to 350° F. for fifteen minutes.
Makes six popovers.

Rye Popovers: Use ¾ cup rye flour and ¼ cup white flour in above recipe.

Whole Wheat Popovers: Use ½ cup whole wheat flour and ½ cup white flour in above recipe.

Surprise Muffins

2 cups flour	1 tablespoon sugar
or { 1 cup flour { 1 cup graham flour	½ teaspoon salt
or { 1 cup flour { 1 cup corn meal	1 cup milk
	2 eggs
3 teaspoons Royal Baking Powder	2 tablespoons shortening, melted

Sift together flour, baking powder, sugar and salt; add milk, well-beaten eggs and melted shortening; mix well. Put table-spoon of batter into each greased muffin tin. Drop into center of each one teaspoon currant, apple or other jelly; or one stewed and sweetened apricot; or one stoned date; or a piece of candied pineapple or other fruit. Add another table-spoon of batter and bake in hot oven at 425° F. twenty to twenty-five minutes.

If graham or corn meal muffins are made, sift flour, baking powder, salt and sugar together and mix in the graham flour or corn meal.

Makes fourteen muffins.

Georgia Sally Lunn

½ cup butter or other shortening	1 cup milk
½ cup sugar	2 cups flour
3 eggs beaten well but not separately	4 teaspoons Royal Baking Powder
	¾ teaspoon salt

Cream butter and sugar well, add eggs and milk a little at a time alternately with the flour which has been sifted with baking powder and salt. Bake in greased shallow pan so that Sally Lunn is about an inch and one-half thick when baked, or in greased muffin pans in hot oven at 425° F. twenty to twenty-five minutes. Break in squares and butter while hot.

Makes ten servings, or if baked in small tins, eighteen muffins.

ROYAL TEA DAINTIES
Pecan Muffins, Brown Sugar Biscuits, Butterscotch Curls

Butterscotch Curls

2 cups flour	4 tablespoons shortening
4 teaspoons Royal Baking Powder	⅔ cup milk
⅔ teaspoon salt	3 tablespoons butter
	½ cup brown sugar

Sift dry ingredients; add shortening, mixing it in with a fork. Add milk to make a fairly soft dough. Knead slightly and roll out about one-fourth inch thick. Spread well with creamed butter and sprinkle with brown sugar. Roll up as for jelly roll and cut in about one-inch pieces. Stand these on end in a well buttered pan, small muffin tins or in muffin rings and bake in a moderate oven at 375° F. for thirty minutes. Centers of rolls curl up and will be glazed on edges.

Makes twelve rolls or twenty-two if baked in small rings.

Green Corn Gems

2 cups golden bantam corn
   cut from cob
¼ cup milk or ½ cup if corn
   is dry
2 eggs

2 cups flour
3 teaspoons Royal Baking Powder
1 teaspoon salt
⅛ teaspoon pepper

Use fresh uncooked corn. Put corn through food chopper; add milk and eggs and beat well; add flour, baking powder, salt and pepper which have been sifted together. Mix and drop into hot greased muffin tins. Bake in moderate oven at 400° F. about twenty-five minutes. Other corn can be used if golden bantam is not available.

Makes sixteen muffins.

Crumpets

2 eggs
1 ½ cups milk
4 tablespoons melted
   shortening

1 teaspoon salt
1 tablespoon sugar
4 teaspoons Royal Baking Powder
2 ½ cups flour

Add beaten eggs and milk to melted shortening and beat well. Add salt, sugar and baking powder sifted with the flour. Put greased muffin rings (large size) on hot slightly greased griddle or frying pan; fill two-thirds full with batter; cook slowly until brown and puffed up; turn with pancake turner and cook other side. Split while hot, butter and serve with cottage cheese.

Makes twelve crumpets.

Pecan Muffins

1 cup graham flour
1 cup flour
4 tablespoons brown sugar
¾ teaspoon salt
4 teaspoons Royal Baking Powder

½ cup chopped pecan nuts
1 cup milk
1 egg
4 tablespoons shortening

Mix together dry ingredients; add nuts, milk, egg and melted shortening and beat well. Put one tablespoon batter into each greased and floured muffin pan or small muffin ring; put half pecan on each muffin and bake in hot oven at 425° F. eighteen to twenty-five minutes, depending on size of muffin.

Makes twelve muffins, or twenty-four if baked in small muffin rings.

Blueberry Muffins

1 cup blueberries
2 cups flour
3 teaspoons Royal Baking Powder
4 tablespoons sugar

½ teaspoon salt
2 eggs
1 cup milk
4 tablespoons shortening

Wash and drain blueberries well; sprinkle with three tablespoons of the measured sugar and a little sifted flour. Sift together remaining dry ingredients; add eggs, milk, melted and cooled shortening to make a stiff batter. Mix in the blueberries. Half fill greased muffin tins and bake in moderate oven at 375° F. for thirty minutes. Canned blueberries carefully drained can be used if fresh berries are not obtainable. Bake in small greased muffin rings for nice variety.

Makes twenty-four small muffins.

Rye Bread Sandwich

Make large loaf of Rye Bread—according to recipe for Rye Rolls, page 18. Knead bread dough as you would for the rolls; allow to stand for a few minutes and bake in round pan so that when finished the bread will be about three or four inches thick, and about the same diameter as ordinary layer cake pan. When bread is cooled, with sharp knife cut off top crust very thin. Slice loaf through into three layers. On first layer spread thick filling of salmon or sardine—made into soft paste with well seasoned mayonnaise. On second layer spread finely chopped egg mixed with mayonnaise, and seasoning. On third layer spread finely chopped olives or pickles. Put on top and spread top and sides of loaf with thick coating of cream cheese which has been softened with a little cream and seasoned well.

Serve whole on lettuce leaves and slice at the table.

Luncheon Surprise

To use with any left-over meat such as lamb, veal, chicken or ham or with well seasoned left-over fish.

Make a biscuit dough as follows:

2 cups flour	4 tablespoons shortening
3 teaspoons Royal Baking Powder	¾ cup milk or half milk and half water
¾ teaspoon salt	

Sift dry ingredients together; mix in the shortening; add the milk to make a soft dough. Roll out *very* thin on floured board and spread with chopped, well seasoned, left-over meat or fish which has been mixed with gravy or sauce. Beginning towards you, roll up just as you would for jelly roll. Bake in hot oven at 475° F. about twenty minutes and serve immediately with gravy or sauce.

Recipe serves six.

Apricot Dessert

½ cup shortening	3 teaspoons Royal Baking Powder
1 cup granulated sugar	¼ teaspoon salt
grated rind ½ orange	¾ cup milk
2 eggs	1 teaspoon vanilla extract
2 cups flour	

Cream the shortening; add the sugar and the grated rind of orange; add well beaten yolks of eggs. Sift together the flour, baking powder and salt and add alternately with the milk; add vanilla; lastly fold in the beaten whites of eggs. Bake in two greased layer cake tins in moderate oven at 350° F. twenty-five minutes.

Spread each layer top and sides with apricot icing, page 89, and put the cake together with sweetened whipped cream.

Eggs à la Surprise

Boil eggs for exactly 3½ minutes. Shell very carefully under water without breaking egg, as it is very soft. Let stand in the boiling water until ready to use.

Have ready circles (about three inches in diameter) of fried bread or toast, in the centers of which a hole has been cut. Set each egg upright in center of each piece of toast. Beat up stiff and dry whites of two or three eggs (depending upon number served); season with salt. Completely cover eggs with this egg white, putting it on roughly but carefully. Take a narrow strip of Spanish pimento and place around the egg about one inch from the top. Place in oven—just long enough for the meringue to brown. Serve hot with Hollandaise or other sauce.

Baked Potatoes with Cheese

Cut baked potatoes in half, lengthwise. Put a thin slice of American cheese on top, sprinkle with salt and paprika. Replace other half of potato and by the time it is served the cheese has melted and makes a delicious luncheon dish.

Corn Soufflé

12 small ears corn	¼ teaspoon pepper
4 eggs	2 tablespoons flour
1 teaspoon sugar	2 tablespoons butter
½ teaspoon salt	1 pint milk
cayenne	2 teaspoons Royal Baking Powder

Cut the corn from the cobs—do not grate it. Add the yolks of eggs beaten lightly, salt, pepper, a dash of cayenne and the butter which has been melted. Beat the egg whites until very light, add the baking powder and beat again. Add to the other ingredients and mix lightly but thoroughly. Pour into greased baking dish, bake in moderate oven at 325° F. forty to fifty minutes

Sweet Potato Puff

4 large sweet potatoes	⅛ cup sugar
¼ cup butter	2 teaspoons Royal Baking Powder
2 well beaten eggs	1 teaspoon salt

Peel potatoes and boil until soft. Mash and add the remaining ingredients. Beat well and put in buttered dish and bake until brown, about one-half hour or more.

Anchovy Eggs

Put eggs in cold water, allow to come to a boil and boil for twenty minutes. Pour off water, allowing to cool in shells. Remove shells and cut each egg in half lengthwise. Remove yolks. Stuff eggs with anchovy paste. Take yolks of eggs, softened with a little butter and seasoning; force through pastry tube around edge of stuffed egg. Put on thin slices of toast and surround with Hollandaise or well seasoned cream sauce. Garnish with strips of pimento.

Broiled Vegetables

For each serving broil the following vegetables which have been previously boiled: Sweet potato cut into slices, two stalks asparagus, one slice egg plant which has been rolled in egg and bread crumbs, and one-half raw tomato and two or three mushrooms that have been peeled.

Arrange on plate with poached egg in center and garnish with parsley.

Lightning Cake

⅓ cup milk	1 cup sugar
2 eggs	¼ teaspoon salt
⅓ cup melted butter	2 cups flour
1 teaspoon vanilla extract	3 teaspoons Royal Baking Powder

Put milk in bowl; add eggs, butter, sugar and vanilla; mix well. Sift flour, salt and baking powder together; add to the liquid ingredients; mix thoroughly. Spread about one inch thick in greased shallow pan, sprinkle with granulated sugar mixed with cinnamon and chopped almonds; bake in moderate oven at 375° F. for about fifteen minutes. When cool, cut or break into squares and serve for luncheon or afternoon tea. For variety one cup chopped nuts or fruit can be added to the dry ingredients.

Makes sixteen squares.

Cake Making

A PERFECT cake! How often have you obtained what you considered a perfect cake? Isn't it often true that one day you will have baked a cake to perfection and the next just a passable cake that your family eats but does not devour with enthusiasm? One layer may be thin, the other thick or humped in the middle or burned on the edges, or again a loaf may have fallen in the center, the icing has hardened before you could spread it or even worse there was insufficient to cover the cake. These are the results that discourage most beginners, but all can be avoided by starting in the right way.

Cake when properly made of good wholesome materials is a nourishing and excellent food. While some prefer a light, fluffy cake and others a moist cake, everyone will agree that to be good a cake must be evenly baked, the crust thin and without cracks and an even brown, the texture fine and even-grained without being close and above all the flavor sweet and delicate.

To always have a perfect result without worry and effort is every woman's ambition and yet it is within her very reach if certain simple rules are followed.

1. Plan so all materials and utensils are at hand when wanted.
2. Choose only the best materials. The best is most economical in the end.
3. Follow directions exactly as given.
4. Be systematic and accurate in all measurements so that results will never vary.
5. Use level measures for all materials.
6. If inexperienced choose a plain cup cake without frosting for your first attempt.
7. Remember that the baking of a cake is as important as the mixing and an oven thermometer is a good investment.
8. Layer cake tins and loaf cake tins come in various sizes, so note how much each recipe makes before deciding on tin to use.
9. All cakes should be baked in the center of the middle shelf—where the heat is uniform. Layer and small cakes should bake quickly in a hot oven and loaf cakes should bake more slowly in a moderate oven.

Standard Butter Cake

⅓ cup butter	1 cup milk
1 cup sugar	2 cups flour
2 eggs	3 teaspoons Royal Baking Powder
1 teaspoon vanilla extract	¼ teaspoon salt

Cream butter thoroughly; add sugar a little at a time, beating well; add yolks of eggs and vanilla; beat well and add the milk a little at a time alternately with the dry ingredients which have been sifted together; mix well but do not beat. Mix in beaten egg whites. Bake in greased and slightly floured loaf tin in moderate oven at 350° F. about forty-five minutes or bake in layer tins or cup cake tins in moderate oven at 375° F. about twenty minutes.

Makes one loaf 8 inches x 4 inches x 3 inches or three eight-inch layers, or sixteen cup cakes.

The following discussion will bring out the important points in all cake making.

Shortening

Butter is preferable for cakes, and unless otherwise specified is the shortening recommended. However, for a white "butter" cake many prefer a white vegetable shortening. Any of the butter substitutes, either solid fats or oils, may of course be used. In molasses cakes and gingerbreads lard will be entirely satisfactory.

Sugar

Granulated is the best sugar for cakes, and if sifted several times will make a fine-grained cake. Powdered sugar also makes a very fine-grained cake, but one that will dry out more quickly as well as a cake slightly less sweet.

Eggs

For all cakes and especially for sponge cakes, always use fresh eggs. There is no difference in food value between white and brown eggs, but the brown eggs make a deeper yellow cake. If fewer eggs are used than specified in a cake recipe, add one-half teaspoon Royal Baking Powder for each egg omitted.

Flour

Either pastry or bread flour can be used in cake making. They can be used in exactly the same amounts. Pastry flour makes a fluffier and more delicate cake and bread flour makes a cake that will keep moist longer. Always sift flour before measuring and again with the baking powder.

High Altitude

At high altitudes external pressure is less than at sea level, so the pressure inside the cake must be less, unless sufficient binding materials such as flour and eggs are used to keep the gas in after it is formed. When baking the standard butter cake at very high altitudes, 7,000 feet or over, reduce the baking powder to two teaspoons and the sugar to three-fourths cup and add one-third cup more flour. In very rich cakes reduce the baking powder, shortening and sugar, or use the same amounts of these ingredients and add slightly more flour or more eggs. For most cakes one teaspoon baking powder will leaven one cup flour, and three-fourths cup sugar will give better results than one cup.

1 SPANISH CAKE—Collect all dry ingredients with necessary utensils for measuring and mixing.

2 Then bring out the liquid ingredients with additional utensils needed.

5 Separate two eggs; first beat the whites until stiff and then without washing the beater beat the yolks.

6 Add to one-half cup milk the liquefied shortening and mix these well with beaten egg yolks.

9 Put into loaf or tube pan, which has been greased and dusted lightly with flour and bake in moderate oven at 350° F. for about 35 minutes.

10 Cake is baked when it shrinks from sides of pan or when a light touch will not leave a depression.

3 Put sifter into mixing bowl and measure into sifter 1¾ cups sifted flour, one cup sugar, three teaspoons Royal Baking Powder, one teaspoon cinnamon, one-quarter teaspoon salt and sift together into bowl.

4 Measure one-half cup butter or other shortening and liquefy by heating over hot water or very low flame—do not cook. This can be melted in a tin measuring cup or small saucepan if held up over flame.

7 Pour the liquid into the dry ingredients and beat well for about two minutes, using an "up and over and under" motion. Keep the batter light and fluffy.

8 Add the egg whites—"cut and fold" them in lightly. Mix them in well without beating.

11 Turn out of pan on to cake cooler over which clean cloth has been placed. When cool turn right side up and cover with Sea Foam Frosting, p. 89. Variations of this recipe follow.

12 Bake in patty pans in moderate oven at 380° F. for 15 minutes; sprinkle with powdered sugar; or bake in layers and spread with chocolate icing; for Cottage Pudding, omit cinnamon and add one teaspoon vanilla or lemon to liquids; bake in ring pan; serve hot with sauce.

1 Gather together all ingredients to be used in foundation recipe.

2 Gather together all utensils needed and grease and lightly flour loaf pan.

5 Measure two cups sifted flour, three teaspoons Royal Baking Powder and one-fourth teaspoon salt and sift together into bowl.

6 Add two eggs, one at a time, to creamed sugar and shortening, beating until batter is very light and fluffy.

9 Fill greased and floured loaf pan three-fourths full and bake in moderate oven at 375° F. for 35 to 45 minutes.

1 MARBLE CAKE—Using same recipe, leave one-third batter in bowl and add one and one-half squares (one and one-half ounces) melted unsweetened chocolate or five tablespoons cocoa mixed with a little cold water.

3 Measure one-half cup—eight tablespoons—shortening or cut one-quarter from a pound print; cream well by softening it with mixing spoon.

4 Measure one cup granulated sugar and add a little at a time, beating until very light and fluffy.

7 Add one teaspoon vanilla extract to batter. Measure two-thirds cup milk. Add a little of the milk to the batter and beat well.

8 Add alternately, a little at a time, the dry ingredients and the rest of milk, mixing well until all is used.

2 Drop chocolate batter into batter in pan, mixing just a trifle to make a "streaky" effect in cake. Bake as directed in step 9.
Other variations follow.

3 FRUIT LOAF—Add to the batter one cup slightly floured raisins or chopped candied fruits. NUT LOAF—Add one cup chopped nuts to the batter. COCOANUT LAYER—Bake in two layer cake tins. Spread layer, top and sides with Cocoanut Icing page 88.

1 For each man take small piece of dough made from gingerbread (page 98); roll with hands into ball; place on greased baking sheet and flatten out to shape the body.

2 For arms take another piece of dough, about one-half the size of first, roll with hands into long round strip and place across top of body, pressing edges well together.

5 Make eyes, nose and mouth with tops and stems of cloves, or with raisins or currants, and then put into moderate oven at 375° F. to bake for twelve minutes.

6 Baked and cooled, their bright colored hats and jackets are made with colored icings. In fact, you can reproduce any popular character by a clever touch here and there.

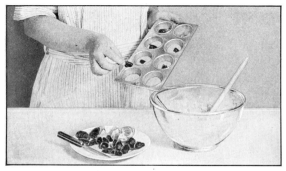

1 SURPRISE MUFFINS—Put one teaspoon Graham Muffin batter into little greased tins; drop pieces of prune, date or candied fruit in center of each.

2 Add another teaspoon of batter and bake in moderate oven at 400° F. about 15 minutes.

3 Take larger piece of dough than in 2, proceed in same way and place on body for legs.

4 For head take small piece of dough, roll into ball flatten and attach to the body at neck; press the edges of dough together.

1 JAM TARTS—Roll out biscuit dough very thin and cut with medium cutter, then cut half the rounds with a slightly smaller cutter.

2 Spread large rounds with butter, place rings on top, fill with jam and bake these as well as the little centers on greased pans in hot oven at 475° F. for 10 minutes.

PRINCESS CAKES—The standard butter cake, page 33, is baked in Princess pans or other small tins. If sprinkled with powdered sugar they will delight the child.

Here they all are, the biscuit centers turned into Fairy Biscuits, Gingerbread Men, Jam Tarts, Princess Cakes and Surprise Muffins.

"Oh, look what mother gave me!"

THE SCHOOL LUNCH BOX

SANDWICHES of home-baked nut and fruit breads, preferably sweetened with molasses—home-made cookies, cup cakes and muffin surprises—with what youthful glee is each new thing in the dainty "mother-packed" lunch box pounced upon and devoured!

In the preparation of the lunch to be carried to school there is a big opportunity for the mother to use her ingenuity in selecting wholesome, nourishing foods of sufficient variety, so that the child welcomes the lunch hour.

We must not forget either that "eating at regular times," whether at home or at school, is a good habit to form, and that, with a little thought and careful planning by the mother, dislikes for certain foods can best be averted when the child is young.

Use eggs, whole milk and butter generously when preparing their recipes and give them foods that will require chewing. Coarse flours are by far the best to use in breads, muffins and cookies.

Carrots are apt to be more popular finely shredded and added to mayonnaise or served with a lemon parsley sauce or combined with gelatin.

Milk served in a small bottle with a straw will suggest a soda.

It is indeed difficult to give variety to a meal for which there is generally so little time for preparation, so it is hoped the following suggestions will help to solve the problem.

THINGS THAT CHILDREN LOVE TO SEE

Cookies made with fancy cutters—animal forms, stars, etc., or shaped with Royal can cover (crescents). A cooky placed atop another with an in-between stuffing of ground raisins, nut butter, jam, or, best of all, ground figs.

For sandwiches instead of ordinary bread, crispy biscuits spread with butter and grated maple or brown sugar are wholesome and especially popular with children.

For cinnamon buns, spread the thinly rolled biscuit dough with butter, sprinkle with cinnamon and plenty of brown sugar; roll like jelly roll, and cut in one and one-half inch slices and bake.

For tarts, roll biscuit dough thin, cut hole in center of one biscuit, place on top of another buttered biscuit, press together; bake and fill with stewed cranberries or other fruit or jam.

WHOLESOME COMBINATIONS
FOR THE SCHOOL LUNCH BOX

Each lunch should include a "meaty" sandwich, a refreshing drink, and a sweet; any of the following with a glass of milk or a cup of hot cocoa makes a light but adequate lunch:

1. Date bread sandwiches spread with butter or cream cheese, peanut cookies, orange.
2. Biscuit sandwiches with chopped chicken, cup custard, cocoanut cookies.
3. Graham biscuit sandwiches with chopped meat filling, doughnuts, baked apple.
4. Brown bread and butter sandwiches, custard cup of baked beans, whole tomato, raisin drop cake.
5. Whole wheat fruit bread sandwiches, cream cheese filling, molasses cookies, tangerine jelly.

PACKING THE LUNCH

The daintiest lunch in the world may be spoiled in the packing. The main thing is to keep the foods separated and so packed that they will not become unwrapped on their way to school.

Cut sandwiches thin and into "lady fingers" or pieces easy to eat, and wrap each in waxed paper. A covered jelly glass or a paper cup nicely holds a baked apple. A custard or chocolate pudding may be packed in the cup in which it is baked.

A thermos bottle is almost indispensable but many lunch boxes come equipped with the bottle as well as the separate containers.

Boston Baked Beans
Brown Bread
Cranberry or Spiced
Fruit Sauce
Milk
Baked Apple Bun

~✤~

Jelly Omelet
Baked Potato—Spinach
Bread and Butter
Milk
Apple Sauce—Fudge Squares
or Brownies

~✤~

Cream of Pea Soup
Chicken Pie
Bread and Butter
Cinnamon Buns
Cocoa

Spinach with Poached Egg,
garnished with Bacon
Milk or Cocoa
Graham Gems
Cottage Pudding
Chocolate Sauce

~✤~

Macaroni and Cheese
Graham Bread
Hot Chocolate
Fruit Jelly, Custard Sauce
Plain Cookies

~✤~

Corned Beef Hash
Vegetable Salad
Muffins
Chocolate Pudding
Milk

Fried Bacon
Creamed Potatoes
Toasted Buttered Biscuits
Glass of Milk
Stewed Prunes
Hot Milk Sponge Cake

~✤~

Puffy Omelet
with Tomato Sauce
Corn Fritters—Raisin Bread
Milk
Cocoanut Cookies

~✤~

Alphabet Soup
Eggs à la Surprise with
Tomato Sauce
Rice Muffins
Cocoa
Individual Cottage Puddings
Fruit Sauce

Doughnuts

The following Doughnuts are made without shortening, and if made with Royal Baking Powder and carefully fried at the proper temperature they will be wholesome and excellent for children.

2 eggs	4 teaspoons Royal Baking Powder
7/8 cup milk	1 cup sugar
3 cups flour	1/2 teaspoon nutmeg
1 teaspoon salt	

Beat eggs until light; add milk, then add this liquid to the dry ingredients, which have been sifted well together. Roll out one-fourth inch thick on slightly floured board, cut out and fry in deep fat at 375° F. Drain well on unglazed paper. Sprinkle with powdered sugar.

Potato Surprise

Bake large potato; cut off top; remove inside; put through ricer; season with salt, pepper and butter; return to shell, leaving a slight depression in center; break an egg carefully on top and return to oven, baking long enough to poach egg. Garnish with parsley;

Cocoanut Cookies

1/4 cup shortening	1 1/2 cups flour
1/2 cup sugar	3 teaspoons Royal Baking Powder
1 egg	
1 teaspoon lemon juice or extract	1/8 teaspoon salt
1/2 cup milk	2 cups fresh grated cocoanut

Cream shortening; add sugar, beaten egg and lemon; mixing milk slowly; add flour, baking powder and salt which have been sifted together. Add cocoanut. Drop by small spoonfuls on greased pan. Do not smooth over, but allow space for spreading. Bake in moderate oven at 385° F. fifteen to twenty minutes.

Makes two dozen cookies.

Scotch Fingers

2 cups rolled oats	1/4 cup milk
1/2 teaspoon salt	1/4 cup molasses
1/4 cup sugar	1 1/2 tablespoons melted butter
3 teaspoons Royal Baking Powder	

Grind rolled oats in the food chopper; mix with salt, baking powder and sugar. Stir in milk, molasses and butter. Mix well. Flour board with ground rolled oats. Roll out in a very thin sheet, and cut into narrow oblong strips. Bake twenty minutes in moderate oven at 375° F.

Makes three dozen.

Cocoa Bread

3 cups flour	6 teaspoons Royal Baking Powder
3 1/2 tablespoons cocoa	
1 teaspoon salt	4 tablespoons honey
1/2 teaspoon cinnamon	7/8 to 1 cup milk

Sift together flour, cocoa, salt, cinnamon and Royal Baking Powder. Mix honey and milk together, add to dry ingredients to make soft dough. Place in greased loaf pan; smooth top and brush with melted butter. Bake in moderate oven at 350° F. for thirty-five minutes. When almost baked, brush top again with milk.

Makes one loaf, 8-in. x 4-in. x 3-in.

Peanut Cookies

1 cup flour	2 tablespoons shortening
1/2 teaspoon salt	1 egg
2 teaspoons Royal Baking Powder	1/4 cup milk
1/2 cup sugar	2 teaspoons lemon juice
	1 cup chopped peanuts

Sift dry ingredients together. Add shortening which has been melted to beaten egg. Add milk and lemon juice, and mix well with the dry ingredients to make soft dough. Add peanuts, mix well and drop by small spoonfuls on greased pan allowing space for spreading. Bake in moderate oven at 375° F. about twenty minutes.

This recipe makes about four dozen small cookies and requires one quart of peanuts.

OTHER RECIPES APPROPRIATE FOR CHILDREN

1 Cream three-fourths cup butter or other shortening well with two cups sugar.

2 Put creamed sugar and shortening aside. Beat two eggs and add one-fourth cup milk.

5 COCOA COOKIES—Take out one-half of dough and put in refrigerator or cool place for future use. Add five tablespoons cocoa to remaining dough and mix well.

6 Add more sifted flour, about one cup, a little at a time and just as much as is necessary to roll out. The softer the dough the richer the cooky will be.

9 Take remaining dough from refrigerator. Add flour, about one cup, a little at a time to make just stiff enough to handle easily. Roll and cut out as desired.

10 Put on greased pan and sprinkle with granulated sugar. A raisin or blanched almond placed on top adds greatly to attractiveness of these cookies. Bake in moderate oven at 380° F. for about 15 minutes.

3 Now mix this liquid slowly in with sugar and shortening and beat well.

4 Add a little at a time, two cups sifted flour, three teaspoons Royal Baking Powder, one-fourth teaspoon nutmeg, one-fourth teaspoon salt which have been sifted together.

7 Take only part of dough at a time and roll out thin or thick as desired; cut out with plain or fancy cutters which have been dipped in flour.

8 Place on greased pan and bake in moderate oven at 375° F. for about 12 minutes.

11 After cookies are removed from oven and cooled, they can be decorated with icing made with four tablespoons confectioner's sugar and a few drops milk. To part of this icing add one teaspoon cocoa to ice the white cookies.

12 The old-fashioned stone cooky jar keeps the cookies fresh for days and cookies, either at meals or between meals, with a glass of milk, are a delight to the children.

1 BROWNIES—Beat two eggs until frothy. Beat in one cup sugar slowly.

2 Melt together over hot water two and one-half squares unsweetened chocolate and one-third cup shortening. Add to egg mixture. Add one-half teaspoon vanilla extract. Mix thoroughly.

5 Cut in squares before removing from pan and while still hot.

1 HERMITS—These are the materials used in this recipe. If desired, the citron and one of the spices may be omitted and result in plainer but very delicious hermits.

4 Sift together into bowl, one and one-half cups sifted flour, two teaspoons Royal Baking Powder, one-fourth teaspoon salt, one teaspoon each cloves, allspice, cinnamon, and add slowly, mixing well.

5 Add one cup chopped seeded raisins, four tablespoons chopped citron which have been dredged with just a little flour.

3 Add one-half cup sifted flour sifted with one-half teaspoon Royal Baking Powder and one-eighth teaspoon salt. Next mix in one cup nuts which have been chopped but not too finely.

4 Spread very thinly on greased and floured shallow baking pan and bake in moderate oven at 325° F. for 30 minutes.

2 These are the utensils used for this recipe. The chopping bowl came from France but is easily obtained here and is most convenient for chopping small quantities.

3 Cream six tablespoons shortening; add one cup brown sugar, one beaten egg. Mix well and add one-fourth cup milk a little at a time.

6 Drop from tip of spoon on greased tin and bake in moderate oven at 375° F. for about twenty minutes.

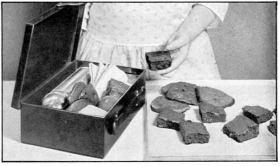

7 A few brownies or hermits are an attractive addition to any lunch box, and the boy or girl taking lunch to school will like to have either included.

1 Assemble the following ingredients. One cup granulated sugar, six eggs, one cup flour, salt, lemon and Royal Baking Powder.

2 These utensils are required. The wire whip is better for a sponge cake than a rotary beater and the spatula, with its pliable blade, is excellent for scraping out bowls.

5 Add grated rind of one-half the lemon which has been washed. Be careful not to grate any of the white skin and scrape all rind from grater.

6 Add two tablespoons lemon juice; mix well and put one side. Now beat the egg whites until very light—use the same whip which has been scraped off, washed and dried.

9 Put in *ungreased* tube pan.

10 Bake in moderate oven at 350° F. for about 50 minutes. The cake should rise in the first 20 minutes; it is baked when it starts to shrink from sides of pan or a light touch with the fingers will not leave an impression.

3 Carefully separate the yolks from the whites of six eggs; put the yolks in one bowl and the whites in another; whip the yolks until very thick and "lemon colored."

4 Sift one cup sugar three times and add gradually to the yolks, whipping until mixture is very light and fluffy and the yolks and sugar thoroughly blended.

7 Add one-half the beaten egg whites to the first mixture and cut and fold in well. Sift one cup flour three times and then sift again with one teaspoon Royal Baking Powder and one-half teaspoon salt.

8 Carefully cut and fold in dry ingredients until mixed well. Then fold in the remaining egg whites.

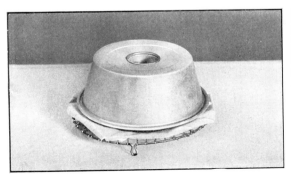

11 Place upside down on cooler over which cloth has been spread and allow to stand until cake cools and gradually drops from pan.

12 Sponge cake is "cut" by separating into pieces with two forks.

The Evolution of Baking Powder

WHEN we bite into a delicate cake or biscuit, it is hard to believe such aristocratic morsels can be the descendants of the sun-baked slabs of grain and water which our primitive ancestors esteemed so highly.

Yet the essential difference between them is the presence of a leavening agent!

Yeast Came First

Very early in written history we come upon mention of both "leavened" and "unleavened" bread, so that the actual origin of raised bread is obscure. Some prehistoric matron, perhaps, was not too careful about washing out the vessel in which she mixed the grain and water for her baking. A stray yeast cell lodged in the scrapings and developed in the next moist mixing, so that the loaf grew astonishingly. It was porous and softer than her ordinary loaves.

She tasted this unusual mass—and found it good. She added a bit of the magic dough to her fresh mixture in the hope that it would impart its characteristics to the new loaves—and of course it did.

Thus began the leavening of grain mixtures, and for generations yeast in some form or other was the only leavening agent known.

Then came pearlash dissolved in vinegar, and later the use of sour milk and bicarbonate of soda. Here was a definite advance. But the addition of a bit too much soda resulted in coarse-grained foods with a yellowish tinge and a most unpleasant taste.

The First Baking Powder

In 1855 "The Practical American Cook Book" published news of a new "portable yeast." This was none other than the combination of soda and cream of tartar! Cakes made with this combination were tender, of delicate texture, and wonderfully delicious.

After some years of experimentation, a really satisfactory quick-acting leavening agent had been discovered—but, alas, not perfected, for these ingredients were not always blended correctly and in the right proportions, making the results uncertain.

But all this disturbing uncertainty was done away with when there was offered to housekeepers a combination of soda and cream of tartar, prepared by careful measure and exact rule, perfectly blended and always ready for instant use. This new leavening agent was called ROYAL BAKING POWDER.

Royal Baking Powder was immediately acclaimed with delight. For it represented a safe and sure way to leaven. A way free from worry, failure, trouble, guess work. It meant that at last the women of the land could cook with the precious certainty that whatever went into the oven would come out right.

Why Royal Became the Standard

Cream of Tartar is the choicest ingredient of which baking powder can be made, for it is a natural fruit acid obtained from fine, ripe grapes. Combined with Tartaric Acid (also a fruit acid derived principally from grapes, although it exists in many other fruits) it makes Royal what is known as a tartrate baking powder.

Both these acids act immediately on the bicarbonate of soda as soon as liquid is added and while the cake or bread mixture is cold, but the Tartaric Acid acts more quickly and the continued action which makes your cake reach its

Public Square at Montpellier, Southern France. The country spreading out from the town wears a mantle of purpling vineyards.

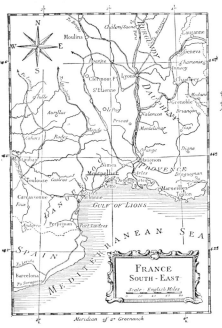

The Department of Herault in Languedoc ranks first in France in the area of its vineyards. At Montpellier, its capital city, the industries are sugar making and fine confectionery, and here it is that Cream of Tartar for Royal Baking Powder is obtained from the juice of the grape.

bined in exactly the correct proportions with pure bicarbonate of soda—so that when the moisture of the batter and the heat of the oven come in contact with them, they will react completely, forming the bubbles of carbon dioxide which make your cakes and biscuits light and digestible. This carbon dioxide is the same gas that makes the bubbles in your glass of ginger ale.

To keep these ingredients dry and to prevent their reacting before entering a batter, cornstarch is added. The Royal Baking Powder Company insures the purity of this cornstarch by manufacturing its own supply.

All these ingredients are thoroughly mixed in dust-proof mixing machines and finally sieved through fine silk bolting cloth so that the final product is absolutely uniform. That is why you can always expect from Royal the same successful and uniform results.

Preferred by Experts

You will find that experts everywhere prefer Cream of Tartar baking powder. Doctors in New England were asked what kind of baking powder they considered most healthful, and 81% of those who answered specified "Cream of Tartar." From doctors in New York State, 83% of the answers were "Cream of Tartar." 82% of answers from Hospital Dieticians throughout the country again said emphatically—"Cream of Tartar baking powder is the most healthful."

4,270 Food Specialists, hundreds of Teachers of Domestic Science, state, "Cream of Tartar baking powder is best."

Authors of 39 authoritative cook books say, "I prefer Cream of Tartar baking powder." And the managers of 76 famous tea rooms, who cannot risk baking failures, say, "We use Royal Baking Powder."

final perfection of lightness in the oven comes from Cream of Tartar, making Royal what is commonly called a "double action" baking powder. This marvelous leavening efficiency of Royal, together with its purity and wholesomeness, have made it the standard throughout the whole world.

No pains are spared to make Royal the ideal leavening agent. To get the Cream of Tartar which it contains, rich, ripe grapes, grown in the famous vineyards that cluster about the Mediterranean, are pressed into juice. This juice is allowed to stand for some time, during which period crystals form—just as they form in a sugar syrup. These crystals are Cream of Tartar, and have the beautiful purple color and rich fragrance of the grapes themselves.

The purple crystals are called "argols." They are shipped to America, where at the plant of the Royal Baking Powder Company they are washed, boiled and recrystallized to remove the color and all impurities. Then they are ground into powder, and are at last ready to be used in Royal Baking Powder.

At autumn, when the grapes are fully ripe, the crop is gathered in. At this season the grape is richest in tartrates.

This refined Cream of Tartar with Tartaric Acid is then com-

1 8-EGG ANGEL CAKE—Separate yolks from whites of eight eggs. Whip whites to a stiff froth. Put yolks away for future use.

2 Whip in one teaspoon cream of tartar. Sift three-fourths cup granulated sugar four times and fold in lightly, adding a small amount at a time.

5 Remove from oven and place on cooler. Angel cake slips from the pan as it cools just as sponge cake does.

1 THREE-EGG ANGEL CAKE—Sift together four times one cup granulated sugar, 1⅓ cups flour, one-half teaspoon cream of tartar, three teaspoons Royal Baking Powder and one-third teaspoon salt.

1 GOLD CAKE—Cream three tablespoons shortening until very light; add slowly three-fourths cup sugar and the yolks of three eggs left from the Angel Cake. Beat up well and add one teaspoon vanilla extract.

2 Finish the Gold Cake by adding one-half cup milk, 1½ cups flour sifted with three teaspoons Royal Baking Powder. Put into a slightly greased and floured pan.

3 Sift together four times three-fourths cup flour, one teaspoon Royal Baking Powder and one-fourth teaspoon salt and add to first mixture, using a folding motion. Add one teaspoon almond extract.

4 Put into ungreased tube pan and bake in slow oven at 300° F., increasing the heat after 30 minutes to 350° F. Bake from 45 to 60 minutes, or until cake shrinks slightly from pan and is a nice light brown.

2 Separate whites from yolks of three eggs. Whip whites until stiff and put the yolks aside for Gold Cake. Scald two-thirds cup milk; cool slightly and add very slowly to the dry ingredients, beating continually.

3 Add one teaspoon vanilla or almond extract; fold in the egg whites and turn mixture into small ungreased tube pan and bake in moderate oven at 350° F. for about 30 minutes.

3 This cake is baked in a moderate oven at 375° F. for 35 minutes. Then it is removed from pan and allowed to cool and, for variety, cut into diamond shaped pieces.

4 The Gold Cake iced with chocolate, white and mocha icings and the Angel Cake iced with boiled frosting are most attractive and inexpensive.

1 JELLY ROLL—Separate two eggs; beat yolks until thick and "lemon color"; add gradually one cup sifted sugar and four tablespoons cold water.

2 Sift one cup sifted flour, one-half teaspoon salt, one teaspoon Royal Baking Powder together, and add a little at a time, mixing well but not beating. Continue using the whip.

5 Spread batter *very thinly* on pan and bake in moderate oven at 350° F. about ten minutes.

6 Turn out immediately on slightly damp cloth sprinkled with powdered sugar.

9 When cool, remove cloth and sprinkle with powdered sugar. This size roll cuts into dainty slices to serve.

1 COCOA CREAM ROLL—Use recipe on page 91 and bake as jelly roll. Trim off crusts and spread with sweetened whipped cream instead of jelly.

3 Now beat up the whites of eggs and fold these carefully but thoroughly into the mixture.

4 Grease one large or two small oblong shallow pans— dust with flour. The smaller pans make rolls easier to handle.

7 With sharp knife quickly trim off any crusty edges.

8 Spread with currant or other jelly and roll up in cloth while still warm. This has to be rather quickly and carefully done.

2 The cocoa roll is better cut into thick slices for serving.

BOSTON CREAM PIE—Use either jelly roll or sponge cake batter. Bake in one deep layer pan in moderate oven at 350° F. for 30 minutes. Split and spread thickly with vanilla cream filling.

Hickory Nut Loaf

1 cup butter	3 teaspoons Royal Baking Powder
1¾ cups sugar	1½ cups chopped hickory, pecan or walnuts
3 eggs	¼ teaspoon salt
¾ cup milk	1 teaspoon vanilla extract
3 cups flour	

Beat butter until soft and creamy; add sugar and yolks of eggs, beating well. Sift flour with baking powder and salt and add alternately, a little at a time with milk. Mix well but do not beat. Add nuts and flavoring; fold in stiffly beaten whites of eggs; mix well. Pour into well-greased and floured loaf pan and bake one hour and forty minutes in moderate oven at 325°F.

Makes one large loaf.

Date Loaf Cake

½ cup butter	1 teaspoon Royal Baking Powder
1 cup brown sugar	1 teaspoon vanilla extract
¾ teaspoon soda	grated rind 1 orange
½ cup milk	1 cup nut meats, chopped
2 cups flour	1 lb. dates, pitted and chopped

Cream butter well, add sugar gradually and beat until light. Dissolve soda thoroughly in the milk. Sift flour with baking powder and add to the creamed mixture, alternately with the milk. Add vanilla, orange rind, nuts and dates. Pour into greased loaf tin and bake in moderate oven at 350° F. for fifty-five minutes.

Makes one small loaf.

Silver Sea Foam Loaf

A Standard White Loaf Cake

½ cup shortening	2 cups pastry flour
1 cup sugar	3 teaspoons Royal Baking Powder
⅔ cup milk	½ teaspoon salt
1 teaspoon almond or vanilla extract	whites of 3 eggs

Cream shortening thoroughly until light and creamy; add sugar a little at a time, beating well; add milk and the flavoring very slowly, beating constantly; stir in the flour, salt and baking powder, which have been sifted together; fold in the whites of eggs which have been beaten until very light. Pour into round greased and floured loaf pan and bake in moderate oven at 350° F. about thirty-five minutes. Cool and cover top and sides of cake with Sea Foam Icing, page 89.

Makes one eight-inch loaf.

Sweet Milk Chocolate Cake

½ cup butter	1 cup milk
2 cups sugar	3 cups pastry flour
4 eggs	½ teaspoon salt
5 squares (5 oz.) sweet milk chocolate	4 teaspoons Royal Baking Powder

Cream butter until very light and fluffy; add sugar a little at a time; add yolks of eggs and chocolate which has been melted; add part of the milk, beating after each addition. Sift flour, salt and baking powder together; add part and the rest of the milk. Beat up the whites of eggs and add half; add the rest of the dry ingredients and the rest of the egg whites. Mix well but do not beat. Pour into greased and floured oblong loaf or tube pan; bake in moderate oven at 350° F. for about forty-five minutes. Spread with Cocoa Icing, page 88.

Makes one large loaf.

Mrs. Moody's Pecan Loaf Cake

6 tablespoons butter	2 cups flour
1 cup sugar	1 teaspoon Royal Baking Powder
3 eggs	½ tablespoon nutmeg, grated
2½ tablespoons lemon and orange juice mixed	2 cups raisins
	2 cups chopped pecans

Cream butter; add sugar slowly. Add beaten egg yolks and beat well. Add lemon and orange juice. Sift flour, Royal Baking Powder and nutmeg. Add nut meats and raisins which have been thoroughly washed and dried. Add to first mixture, mixing in well. Mix in egg whites beaten until stiff. Bake in well greased tube pan about one hour in slow oven at 250° F., then increase heat to 325° F. and bake fifteen minutes longer.

Makes one nine-inch loaf.

Coffee Fruit Cake

½ cup butter	¼ teaspoon salt
1 cup light brown sugar	⅓ cup strong, cold coffee
3 eggs	¼ cup milk
2¼ cups flour	1 cup raisins
3 teaspoons Royal Baking Powder	½ cup sliced citron
	½ cup figs, cut in strips

Cream butter; add sugar slowly; add well beaten eggs, mixing well. Sift together flour, baking powder and salt and add a little at a time alternately with coffee and milk. Add fruit, which has been slightly floured and put in greased and floured tube loaf pan. Bake in moderate oven at 350° F. for fifty minutes. Sift powdered sugar over top.

Makes one eight-inch loaf.

Luxor Loaf

1 cup fine granulated sugar	⅛ teaspoon baking soda
1 teaspoon vanilla extract	1½ cups pastry flour
½ cup egg yolks	2 teaspoons Royal Baking Powder
½ cup lukewarm water	½ teaspoon salt

Sift the sugar, pour the vanilla extract on 2 tablespoons of the measured sugar, and set aside.

Place egg yolks in a large mixing bowl; add water and baking soda and beat with egg beater until very foamy.

Add sugar a little at a time, beating in well. Add the sugar mixed with the flavoring and beat in well.

Sift together the flour, baking powder and salt and fold carefully into the mixture. Pour in large ungreased angel cake pan. Bake in moderate oven at 350° F. for 40 to 45 minutes. Invert pan and cake and let stand until cake is cold when, with the aid of a spatula it will slip from the pan. Remove all crumbs and moist crust from surface and cut in three layers. Spread Lemon Filling, page 89, between the layers. Cover top and sides with Marshmallow Seven Minute Frosting, page 88.

Makes one large loaf.

Royal Cream Loaf Cake

½ cup butter	½ cup rich milk or thin cream
1 cup sugar	1 cup bread flour
2 eggs	½ cup cornstarch
1 teaspoon lemon extract	3 teaspoons Royal Baking Powder

Cream butter; add sugar slowly; add beaten yolks of eggs and flavoring; add milk a little at a time; sift flour, cornstarch and baking powder together and add; fold in beaten whites of eggs. Bake in greased loaf pan in moderate oven at 375° F. thirty-five to forty-five minutes and cover with white frosting, page 88.

Makes one small loaf.

Sunshine Cake

6 eggs	1 teaspoon Royal Baking
⅛ teaspoon salt	Powder
1¼ cups granulated sugar	½ teaspoon vanilla extract
6 tablespoons cold water	½ teaspoon almond extract
1 cup sifted flour	

Separate yolks and whites of eggs. Beat whites stiff, adding salt. Cook sugar and water until syrup spins a thread when dropped from spoon. Pour while hot over egg whites and beat till cool, as for boiled icing. Beat yolks until thick, add one-half teaspoon baking powder to yolks and other half to the flour (sifted at least four times). Add flavoring. Blend all together with the whites. Pour into ungreased angel food tube pan and bake fifty minutes. Start in slow oven at 300° F., increase to 350° F., and last part of baking decrease the heat again. To cool, invert pan.

Makes one nine-inch loaf.

Betty's Feather Sponge Cake

6 eggs (6 yolks and 3 whites)	2¾ cups bread flour
2 cups granulated sugar	4 teaspoons Royal Baking
juice and rind of 1 lemon	Powder
1 cup boiling water	

Separate eggs. Put whites one side and beat the yolks until very thick and light lemon color. Sift granulated sugar and add a little at a time, beating continually; add the grated rind and juice of one lemon, being careful not to grate in any of the white skin; add boiling water a little at a time and beat the batter until very light and fluffy, about ten minutes. Sift flour and baking powder and fold these dry ingredients in the batter; now beat up the egg whites and fold the whites in last, mixing them in well but do not beat. Pour batter in very thin layer into well greased and floured shallow baking pan. Sprinkle with powdered sugar and put into a moderate oven at 385° F. This cake will take about twenty-five minutes to bake and should be a very light golden brown on top and shrink slightly from the sides of the pan. Allow to cool and break apart with forks into small pieces for serving. This sponge cake will keep moist and fresh for several days.

Makes one large sheet—24 servings.

Dutch Apple Cake

2 cups flour	1 egg
3 teaspoons Royal Baking Powder	⅔ cup water
1 tablespoon sugar	4 apples
½ teaspoon salt	½ cup sugar
4 tablespoons shortening	2 teaspoons cinnamon

Sift flour, baking powder, sugar and salt together. Add shortening, mixing in with a fork. Beat egg, add water. Add to dry ingredients to make soft dough. Spread one-half inch thick in greased pie plate or baking pan. Wash, pare, core and cut apples into eighths. Press into dough, placing close together. Dot with small pieces of butter. Mix sugar and cinnamon together and sprinkle on apples and top of cake. Bake in moderate oven at 350° F. for about twenty-five minutes or until apples are tender. Serve hot with hard sauce, cream or the following

Lemon Sauce

1 cup sugar	1 tablespoon butter
⅓ cup water	4 teaspoons lemon juice

Boil sugar and water together five minutes or until syrupy. Add butter and lemon juice.

Makes one eight-inch cake.

Hot Milk Sponge Cake

4 eggs	1 cup flour
1 cup sugar	¼ teaspoon salt
6 tablespoons hot milk	1½ teaspoons Royal Baking Powder
1 tablespoon lemon juice	
Grated rind of ½ lemon	

Beat egg yolks until thick; add half the sugar, beating continually; add hot milk, remainder of sugar and beaten egg whites; add lemon juice and rind; add flour, salt and baking powder which have been sifted together. Bake in ungreased tube pan in moderate oven at 350° F. about forty-five minutes.

Makes one eight-inch loaf.

Mrs. Gray's Spice Filled Coffee Cake

3 cups sifted flour	¼ teaspoon cinnamon
4 teaspoons Royal Baking Powder	¾ cup sugar
1 teaspoon salt	¼ cup butter
¼ teaspoon mace or nutmeg	2 eggs
	1 cup milk

Sift flour; measure. Sift again with baking powder, salt, mace, cinnamon and sugar. Work in butter with finger tips. Add eggs, unbeaten, and milk. Stir to a smooth dough. Turn into a well oiled round cake pan and cover with the following

Top Mixture

¼ cup butter	½ teaspoon cinnamon
¾ cup brown sugar	⅛ teaspoon salt
3 tablespoons flour	¾ cup almonds, cut in small pieces

Cream the butter, add the brown sugar and flour. Cream together well. Add the cinnamon and salt. Spread over the top of the coffee cake. Scatter almonds over this. Bake twenty-five minutes in a moderate oven at 375° F. When cool, split cake in half and put a layer of sweetened whipped cream over the bottom half of the cake. Cover with upper half of cake and serve, cutting sections as for pie.

Makes one eight-inch cake.

Upside Down Cake

⅓ cup butter	1½ cups flour
⅔ cup sugar	3 teaspoons Royal Baking Powder
2 eggs	⅛ teaspoon salt
½ teaspoon vanilla extract	⅔ cup water

Cream butter; add sugar. Add beaten egg yolks and vanilla. Sift together flour, baking powder and salt. Add to first mixture alternately with water. Fold in stiffly beaten egg whites.

While making the cake, melt four tablespoons butter and one cup brown sugar in frying pan or dripping pan. When thick and syrupy arrange in syrup slices of canned pineapple or halves of fresh or canned peaches or two cups of any fruit cut in small pieces. Pour in the batter and bake in moderate oven at 375° F. for about thirty-five minutes. Remove at once to dish, turning upside down so that the fruit will be on top. Serve hot with hard sauce or whipped cream.

Makes one nine-inch cake.

Mrs. Moody's Gingerbread

2 cups molasses	3 cups sifted bread flour
¾ cup butter	1 cup buttermilk (or sour milk)
2 teaspoons baking soda	
1 teaspoon powdered ginger	1 egg, beaten very light
½ teaspoon cinnamon	4 teaspoons Royal Baking Powder
half grated nutmeg	

Bring molasses and butter to boiling point. Stir in baking soda, ginger, cinnamon and nutmeg. Remove from fire and add sifted bread flour and buttermilk (or sour milk) alternately. Add egg and baking powder. Put in buttered and warmed small tins or on baking sheet. Bake in moderate oven at 350° F. fifteen minutes.

Makes twenty-four small cakes.

1   Half fill frying kettle with lard, oil or other cooking fat and put over low flame to heat.

2   Line dripping pan with clean unglazed paper and put aside ready to drain doughnuts.

5   Add enough more flour to roll. Roll out part of dough at a time on slightly floured board to about one-half inch thick. Cut with doughnut cutter first dipped in flour. If dough is chilled before rolling it will be easier to handle.

6   Test fat with thermometer. When temperature reaches 375° F. it is ready for frying doughnuts. If doughnuts are thicker than one-fourth inch they will require a lower temperature, 370° F. If fat is not hot enough grease will be absorbed and if too hot doughnuts will crack.

9   Doughnuts will puff up and rise to surface as they cook. When brown on one side, turn and brown other side, cooking thoroughly. It should take about two minutes to fry doughnuts.

10   Drain well, then put on prepared paper to drain again.

3 Cream three tablespoons butter or other shortening with two-thirds cup sugar and add one beaten egg.

4 Sift together three cups flour, three-fourths teaspoon salt, one teaspoon nutmeg, four teaspoons Royal Baking Powder, and add part to the first mixture. Add two-thirds cup milk slowly; then add remainder dry ingredients.

7 If you have no thermometer, test temperature with small cube of bread. Drop the bread in fat; if it browns in 60 seconds it is just hot enough.

8 Place as many doughnuts in basket as will just cover bottom and lower basket in fat, or drop them into the fat and as they come to the surface see that they do not overlap.

11 Sprinkle with powdered sugar just before serving.

12 Croquettes and codfish balls or any previously cooked foods are fried in exactly the same way only at a higher temperature, 385° F., or allowing 40 seconds to brown the bread in bread test.

Deep Fat Frying

Utensils

A large iron frying kettle with wire basket that hangs on hooks attached to sides of kettle is best for deep fat frying. When not available a deep saucepan and wire spoon, strainer or egg whip may be used for draining off the fat.

A pan or platter on which is unglazed paper, that will absorb grease, for draining all fried food is necessary and should be kept in a warm place during the frying.

Preparation of Food for Frying

Potatoes should be well dried before lowering into fat and only sufficient to cover basket fried at one time. If any water is left in food it will sputter as soon as put into the fat.

Fry only a few doughnuts, croquettes, or other foods at one time.

Croquettes, pieces of fish, etc., are shaped and then rolled in bread crumbs, egg and crumbs, or they are rolled in flour, egg and then flour before frying. Fruits, vegetables, filets of fish or chicken, oysters, clams and smelts are also added to a batter, and then fried in deep fat.

Fritter Batter

1 cup flour	¼ teaspoon salt
1½ teaspoons Royal Baking Powder	1 egg
	⅔ cup milk

Sift flour, baking powder and salt together into bowl. Add egg which has been beaten and the milk. Beat until smooth and fry as directed.

Vegetable Fritters

Cut into small pieces cooked cauliflower, eggplant, oyster-plant, and string beans. Put in plain fritter batter and fry in deep fat hot enough to brown a piece of bread in forty seconds, at 385° F.

Apple Fritters

4 large apples	1 tablespoon lemon juice
2 tablespoons powdered sugar	

Peel and core apples and cut into slices; add sugar and lemon juice. Add to fritter batter and fry by spoonfuls in deep fat hot enough to brown a piece of bread in sixty seconds, at 375° F. Fry a light brown and drain on unglazed paper. Sprinkle with cinnamon and powdered sugar and serve immediately. Makes eighteen fritters.

Fruit Fritters

Fruits other than apples may be used in fritters by following the directions for apple fritters. Canned whole fruits drained from syrup may also be used. Chop fruit (not too fine) and stir into plain fritter batter. Drop by spoonfuls into deep hot fat, turning until brown. Drain and sprinkle with powdered sugar.

French Fried Vegetables

Pieces of eggplant, summer squash, cauliflower and parsnip, parboiled and drained, may be dipped in flour, egg, and flour and fried in deep hot fat at 385° F.

Fat

The vegetable oils are perhaps the easiest to use and best for frying. Solid fats as lard, any of the solid vegetable fats, and a mixture of lard and suet are also good. The frying kettle should be about half filled with fat—no more. All fat should be strained through cheese cloth directly after using and kept covered in a cold place until needed.

To Test Temperature of Fat

Drop a small cube of bread in fat and count the number of seconds it requires to brown. Consult temperature tables on page 11 for the proper temperatures for the different foods.

Uncooked foods such as fish and doughnuts, will require a longer time to cook and should be fried at a lower temperature than croquettes, codfish balls or other cooked foods.

Thin pieces of food should be fried at a higher temperature than thick pieces. Don't attempt to fry in deep fat any very thick pieces of food as they will require so low a temperature in order to cook thoroughly that grease will be absorbed.

French Fried Chicken

Select very young chicken, weighing from 1 to 1½ lbs.; thoroughly wash and dry, and rub with salt and pepper; cut in quarters. Dip in egg and then in flour to which Royal Baking Powder has been added (½ teaspoon Royal to 2 tablespoons flour), and fry in hot deep fat at 345° to 355° F. 8 to 10 minutes.

If desired, the chicken may be dipped in a plain, fritter batter and fried at 355° F. for 8 minutes.

Corn Fritters

½ cup milk	⅛ teaspoon pepper
2 cups boiled corn cut from cob	3 teaspoons Royal Baking Powder
2 cups flour	1 tablespoon melted shortening
1½ teaspoons salt	2 eggs

Add milk to corn; add flour sifted with salt, pepper and baking powder; add shortening and well-beaten eggs. Beat all together and fry by spoonfuls in fat hot enough to brown a piece of bread in sixty seconds, at 375° F. Drain well on unglazed paper and serve immediately. Makes eighteen fritters.

Clam Fritters

1½ cup flour	½ cup milk or clam juice
2 teaspoons Royal Baking Powder	2 eggs
½ teaspoon salt	1½ teaspoons grated onion
⅛ teaspoon pepper	1 teaspoon melted shortening
⅛ teaspoon paprika	10 clams

Sift together dry ingredients; add liquid, beaten eggs, onion and shortening; rinse clams, put through meat chopper and add to batter. Take one spoonful batter for each fritter and fry in deep fat hot enough to brown a piece of bread in sixty seconds, at 375° F. Drain and serve immediately. Makes sixteen fritters.

Banana Fritters

3 bananas	1 tablespoon lemon juice
2 tablespoons sugar	

Force bananas through sieve; add sugar and lemon juice and add to fritter batter; beat thoroughly. Drop by spoonfuls into deep fat hot enough to brown a piece of bread in sixty seconds, at 375° F. Drain on unglazed paper and sprinkle with powdered sugar. Serve with a few drops of lemon juice or lemon sauce. Makes eighteen fritters.

Codfish Balls

1 cup salt codfish	1/8 teaspoon pepper
2 cups potatoes, cut into cubes or small pieces	1/2 tablespoon butter
	1 egg

Pick over, wash and shred fish. Put potatoes into deep saucepan; cover with cold water; add fish and boil until potatoes are soft. Take off fire; drain well; beat with fork until light and all lumps are out; add seasoning, butter and slightly beaten egg. Drop by spoonfuls into deep fat hot enough to brown a piece of bread in forty seconds at 385° F. and fry until golden brown. Drain on paper and serve immediately.

Makes twelve codfish balls.

Nut and Potato Croquettes

2 cups hot riced potatoes	Few grains cayenne
1/4 cup milk	Yolk of 1 egg
1 teaspoon salt	1/2 cup pecan nut meats, chopped not too fine
1/8 teaspoon pepper	

Mix all ingredients with fork until light. Shape into small croquettes. Roll in bread crumbs. Dip in egg which has been mixed with a little cold water. Roll in bread crumbs again and fry a golden brown in deep fat hot enough to brown a piece of bread in forty seconds at 385° F. Drain on unglazed paper and serve.

Makes twelve croquettes.

Chicken Croquettes

2 tablespoons butter	1/8 teaspoon paprika
2 tablespoons flour	1/8 teaspoon pepper
1 cup milk	1 tablespoon chopped parsley
2 teaspoons salt	
1 teaspoon Worcestershire sauce, if desired	2 cups chopped chicken
	2 eggs

Melt butter in saucepan; add flour and cold milk slowly, stirring until smooth and creamy; add seasoning and parsley. Boil three minutes. Add chicken; mix well and pour out on platter to cool. When cool enough to handle take a large spoon of the mixture in floured hands; shape into balls, cones or oval cakes and put into cold place until firm. Roll in bread crumbs, then in eggs beaten with two tablespoons cold milk, then in the bread crumbs. Fry in deep fat hot enough to brown a piece of bread in forty seconds at 385° F. and drain on brown paper.

Makes fourteen croquettes.

Afternoon Tea Crullers

2 eggs	2 tablespoons melted shortening
6 tablespoons sugar	6 tablespoons milk
3/4 teaspoon salt	2 1/2 cups flour
1/4 teaspoon grated nutmeg	3 teaspoons Royal Baking Powder

Beat eggs until light and then add sugar, salt, nutmeg, shortening and milk, beating continually. Add two cups flour which has been sifted with the baking powder; then add more flour to roll on board without sticking. Roll out to about one-fourth inch thick. Cut into strips about four inches long and about one-half inch wide. Twist some of these strips by bringing the ends together as in making ordinary crullers. Make others into single twists and into any shape desired. They should be much smaller than ordinary crullers or doughnuts. Fry in deep fat at 385° F. until light golden brown. Drain thoroughly on unglazed paper and just before serving, sprinkle with powdered sugar.

This recipe makes about sixty small crullers or twists.

Rice Croquettes

1 cup rice	1 tablespoon sugar
2 eggs	1 tablespoon butter
3 tablespoons milk	1 teaspoon chopped parsley
1 teaspoon salt	

Wash rice several times and boil with two quarts boiling water thirty minutes. Drain well and put into top of double boiler. Add one egg beaten with two tablespoons milk, salt, sugar, butter and parsley; cook until egg thickens. Cool and shape into cones, balls or oval cakes. Roll in crumbs, dip into egg beaten up with one tablespoon milk and roll in bread crumbs. Fry in deep fat hot enough to brown a piece of bread in forty seconds at 385° F.

Makes twelve croquettes.

French Fried Potatoes

Peel potatoes and slice in rather thin long pieces. Put into cold water for a few minutes. Drain and dry well. Fry in deep fat hot enough to brown a cube of bread in twenty seconds at 395° F. Potatoes will take about twenty minutes to cook unless cut in very thin pieces. Drain on brown paper and salt just before serving.

Sweet Potatoes can be fried in same way.

Saratoga Chips are cut very thin with special cutter and fried as above, only for a much shorter time.

Julienne are similar to French Fried, only cut in short thin pieces with special cutter, as are also *Latticed Potatoes.*

Potato Croquettes

3 cups hot riced potatoes	pepper and salt
1 tablespoon butter	few teaspoons milk
1 egg	

Mix all together lightly with fork. Cool and shape into Croquettes. Roll in egg and cracker crumbs or bread crumbs and fry in deep fat hot enough to brown bread in forty seconds, at 385° F. Drain well and serve garnished with parsley.

Makes about twelve croquettes.

Mrs. Moody's Doughnuts

3 eggs	1/8 teaspoon salt
1 cup sugar	4 1/2–5 cups flour
3 tablespoons melted butter	3 teaspoons Royal Baking Powder
1 cup milk	
1 teaspoon nutmeg	

Beat the eggs. Add the sugar and the melted butter. Add the milk and nutmeg and salt. Mix with flour, with which the baking powder has been sifted, to make a soft dough. Roll out to one-half inch thick. Cut with small doughnut cutter and fry in deep fat at 375° F. to a light brown. Drain and roll in powdered sugar.

Makes five dozen doughnuts.

Jam Turnovers

2 cups flour	1 tablespoon sugar
4 teaspoons Royal Baking Powder	2 tablespoons melted butter
1/2 teaspoon salt	2/3 cup milk

Sift dry ingredients. Add butter and milk and mix all together well. Roll out thin; cut in rounds with lid of baking powder tins; put some jam in center of each. Moisten edges with milk and fold over like turnover. Pinch edges well together, fry in deep fat at 365° F. until brown.

Makes sixteen.

1 CREAM PUFFS—Put one cup boiling water and one-half cup shortening together in saucepan; boil up well and add all at once one cup sifted flour which has been sifted with one-eighth teaspoon salt and stir vigorously.

2 Remove from fire as soon as mixed; cool; mix in three eggs, one at a time.

5 Cut near the base of each puff to admit the filling. Use vanilla cream filling on page 89. Puffs can be served plain, sprinkled with powdered sugar or iced with chocolate, white or coffee icing.

6 The same puffs can be filled with whipped cream, or when strawberries are in season mix the cream with crushed and sweetened strawberries and a delightful dessert is the result.

Tiny Puffs for reception or afternoon tea can be made, using the same pastry bag. These little puffs take a shorter time to bake and are new and very dainty.

Eclairs and puffs are sometimes split and filled with chicken salad and are served on lettuce leaves.

3 Add two teaspoons Royal Baking Powder and beat well. Drop by spoonfuls 1½ inches apart on greased tin.

4 Shape with wet spoon into circular form. Put into a hot oven at 450° F. and after 10 minutes reduce the heat to 400° F., baking about 25 minutes, or until puffed up, light brown and thoroughly cooked.

1 ECLAIRS—For eclairs use same cream puff mixture and force through pastry bag. Eclairs are baked exactly as cream puffs.

2 These eclairs are filled with either chocolate, vanilla, or coffee cream and iced with white, chocolate and coffee icing.

Ice-cream filled puff with chocolate sauce.

Small puffs are delicious filled with seasoned cream cheese and are served as an accompaniment to salad.

1 BOILED FROSTING—Put one cup granulated sugar, one-half cup cold water in saucepan over low flame. Stir until dissolved. Continue cooking slowly without stirring.

2 While syrup is cooking beat the white of one egg until stiff but not too dry.

5 Add one-half teaspoon flavoring extract and one-half teaspoon Royal Baking Powder and beat until stiff enough to spread. Spread on cold cake with spatula. The icing should be thick enough to "pile up" on cake.

1 SEVEN MINUTE FROSTING—Put seven-eighths cup granulated sugar, three tablespoons cold water, one unbeaten egg white, into top of double boiler.

1 BUTTER ICING—Put one-half cup butter (part substitute can be used) in bowl and cream thoroughly with wooden spoon.

2 Mix in one egg yolk, or if white icing is desired, only white of egg. The yolk gives a very soft shade.

3 Put a candy thermometer in syrup. When syrup reaches 238° F. remove from fire.
If you have no thermometer test by dropping syrup from spoon. When it leaves a long fine, hairlike thread it is done.

4 Pour syrup slowly over beaten egg white, beating continually either with egg beater or spoon.

2 Place over boiling water and beat with dover beater for exactly seven minutes.

3 Remove from fire. Add one-half teaspoon flavoring extract and one-half teaspoon Royal Baking Powder. Beat well until of right consistency to spread. This icing can be spread on hot or cold cake.

3 Gradually work in three cups confectioner's sugar, beating until very smooth and fluffy.

4 Add one teaspoon vanilla extract and few drops of hot cream if necessary to make icing of good consistency for spreading on cold cake.

Pinwheel Cookies

½ cup butter	1½ cups flour
½ cup sugar	1½ teaspoons Royal Baking Powder
1 egg yolk	⅛ teaspoon salt
3 tablespoons milk	½ teaspoon vanilla extract
1 square (1 oz.) chocolate, melted	

Cream butter, add gradually the sugar, add egg yolk and beat the mixture well. Add the milk; add the flour which has been sifted with the baking powder and salt. Add vanilla extract. Divide dough into halves. To one-half of this mixture add melted chocolate.

Roll the white dough into a thin rectangular sheet, then roll the chocolate mixture into a sheet the same size. Place white dough over the chocolate and gently press together.

Roll up as for jelly roll into a tight roll about 2 inches in diameter. Set in ice-box for several hours to become firm. Cut into one-fourth inch (thin) slices with a sharp knife and lay, cut side down, on a greased cooky sheet. Bake in a moderate oven at 375° F. for about eight to ten minutes.

Makes four dozen cookies.

Almond Macaroons

¼ cup almond paste	few grains salt
1 cup powdered sugar	3 egg whites
1 teaspoon Royal Baking Powder	

Work together the almond paste, salt, baking powder and sugar. Beat the egg whites very stiff and add to the paste, using a spatula or wooden spoon. Mix until perfectly smooth. Put heavy oiled paper or a sheet of heavy brown paper covered with a sheet of thin oiled paper on a baking sheet and drop the mixture on it by small spoonfuls or force it through a paper pastry tube, placing them about one inch apart. Decorate with bits of cherry, nuts, angelica or candied peel. Bake until very delicately browned (about thirty minutes) in a slow oven at 300° F.

Makes fifty small macaroons

Nut Bars

½ cup shortening	4 cups flour
1½ cups sugar	3 teaspoons Royal Baking Powder
2 eggs	
1 teaspoon almond or lemon extract	¼ teaspoon salt
4 tablespoons milk	½ cup blanched almonds, split in halves

Cream shortening and sugar together; add beaten yolk of one egg; add beaten whites of two eggs, flavoring and three tablespoons milk; mix well. Sift together flour, baking powder and salt and add, mixing well. Roll half of dough at a time, one-fourth-inch thick on flour board; cut into bars one by three inches. Brush with remaining yolk of egg mixed with one tablespoon milk. Place halved almonds on top. Bake in moderate oven at 400° F. fifteen minutes.

Makes eight dozen.

Rochester Ginger Snaps

1 cup molasses	1 teaspoon ginger
1 cup sugar	½ teaspoon soda
½ cup butter	1 egg
1 teaspoon cinnamon	2 cups flour
	1 teaspoon Royal Baking Powder

Boil together molasses, sugar, butter, spices and soda for five minutes. Cool and add the egg, beaten, and flour sifted with baking powder. Roll very thin on floured board and cut in strips one inch wide and about four inches long. Place on greased baking pans or cooky sheet and bake in moderate oven at 400° F. for six minutes.

Makes eight dozen ginger snaps.

Meringues

whites of 3 eggs	3 teaspoons Royal Baking Powder
1¼ cups granulated sugar	¼ teaspoon vanilla extract

Beat whites of eggs until stiff and dry; add gradually two-thirds of sugar and continue beating until mixture holds shape; fold in remaining sugar sifted with baking powder; add vanilla. Drop by spoonfuls on unglazed paper and bake in slow oven at 250° F. thirty minutes. Increase heat to 300° F. and bake thirty minutes longer. Remove any soft part from center of meringues and return to oven to dry out, after turning off heat. Use two meringues for each serving and put together with ice cream or with sweetened whipped cream and crushed raspberries or strawberries.

Makes eighteen.

Shortbreads Royal

6 tablespoons butter	2 cups flour
1 cup sugar	½ teaspoon salt
2 eggs	¼ teaspoon Royal Baking Powder
1 teaspoon vanilla extract	

Cream the butter and sugar, then add the beaten eggs and flavoring. Mix and sift the dry ingredients and add to the first mixture. Mix well. Knead slightly and roll on floured board to about one-fourth inch thick. Use two pastry cutters of different sizes, also one tiny round cutter, preferably a thimble. First, cut out a large round for the base, then a smaller size for the top. With the thimble, cut three holes from the top round. Spread the large round with jam and over this lay the smaller one so that the jam is visible through the holes. Brush top with a little egg yolk and sprinkle with sugar. Bake in a moderate oven at 385° F. for about twenty minutes.

Makes twelve to fourteen.

Mrs. Moody's Black Walnut Bars

2 eggs	¾ cup flour
1 cup sugar	¾ teaspoon Royal Baking Powder
½ cup butter	
2 sq. unsweetened chocolate, melted	1 teaspoon vanilla extract
	1 cup black walnut pieces

Break eggs into bowl large enough for entire ingredients. Beat well with egg beater. Add sugar slowly and mix well. Have chocolate and butter melted together and add to egg and sugar mixture.

Sift flour with baking powder and add with vanilla. Mix all together and add nuts (dredged with a little of the flour). Bake in greased shallow pan in thin sheets in moderate oven at 350° F. for fifteen minutes. Spread with the following

Chocolate Icing

White of one egg, unbeaten, three-fourths cup confectioner's sugar and three tablespoons melted chocolate. Stir together and add boiling water if necessary. Spread on the baked sheets as soon as they come out of the oven. Cut into bars about three inches by three-quarters inch.

Makes six dozen.

Oatmeal Macaroons

1 cup sugar	2½ cups rolled oats
1 tablespoon melted shortening	2 teaspoons Royal Baking Powder
2 eggs	
¾ teaspoon salt	1 teaspoon vanilla extract

Mix sugar with shortening; add yolks, salt and rolled oats; add baking powder, beat egg whites and vanilla; mix thoroughly. Drop on greased tins about half teaspoon to each macaroon, allowing space for spreading. Bake about ten minutes in moderate oven at 350° F.

Makes three dozen.

Blueberry Tea Cake

5 tablespoons shortening	1 ¾ cups flour
1 cup sugar	3 teaspoons Royal Baking Powder
2 eggs	1 ½ cups blueberries
⅔ cup milk	

Cream shortening; add sugar, beaten eggs and milk; sift flour and baking powder and add, mixing well. Stir in blueberries, which have been rolled in a little of the measured sugar and flour. Bake in shallow greased and floured pan in moderate oven at 375° F. about twenty-five minutes. Break in small pieces and serve hot with butter.

Makes one sheet cake 12″ x 8″ x 1″.

Hot Molasses Cake

½ cup shortening	¼ teaspoon soda
½ cup brown sugar	½ teaspoon salt
1 egg	½ teaspoon allspice
¼ cup molasses	1 teaspoon cinnamon
2 cups flour	½ cup milk
3 teaspoons Royal Baking Powder	

Cream shortening well; add sugar slowly, beating continually; add beaten egg; beat well and add molasses; add half of flour, baking powder, salt, soda and spices, which have been sifted together; add milk and remainder of dry ingredients. Mix well. Bake in greased shallow pan in hot oven at 425° F. about twenty minutes. Serve hot with butter.

This is delicious with whipped cream or chocolate icing.

Makes a sheet of Molasses Cake 8″ x 12″ x 1″.

Nun's Cake

1 cup butter	2 ½ teaspoons Royal Baking
1 ½ cups powdered sugar	Powder
yolks of 5 eggs	3 teaspoons caraway seeds
whites of 2 eggs	¼ teaspoon salt
¾ cup milk	1 teaspoon rose extract
3 cups pastry flour	½ teaspoon extract cinnamon

Beat butter until soft and creamy; add sugar and yolks of eggs, beating well. Stir in unbeaten whites of eggs and beat one minute. Sift flour with baking powder and salt and add alternately, a little at a time with milk. Mix well but do not beat. Sprinkle in caraway seeds and flavoring; mix well. Pour into well-greased and floured loaf pan and bake one hour and forty minutes in moderate oven at 325° F.

Makes one loaf about 7 ½″ in diameter and 3 ½″ high.

Fig Cake

¾ cup butter	4 teaspoons Royal Baking Powder
1 ½ cups sugar	whites of 4 eggs
1 cup milk	1 teaspoon lemon extract
3 cups pastry flour	½ teaspoon salt

Cream butter and sugar; add milk. Sift flour, salt and baking powder; add one-half of the flour, then well-beaten egg whites, then rest of flour and extract.

Take two-thirds of the mixture and add one teaspoon cinnamon, one teaspoon nutmeg, 1 ½ cups finely cut and floured figs and one tablespoon of molasses.

Put in a greased and lightly floured round tube pan a spoonful of light mixture and then a spoonful of dark mixture alternately as for marble cake. Bake in moderate oven at 350° F. Increase heat to 360° F. and last half-hour decrease to 350° F. Bake about fifty-five minutes.

Makes one eight-inch loaf.

Feather Cocoanut Cake

1 ½ cups pastry flour	1 egg
⅞ cup sugar	½ cup milk
4 teaspoons Royal Baking Powder	1 teaspoon lemon extract
4 tablespoons melted shortening	½ cup fresh grated cocoanut

Sift together flour, sugar and baking powder. Add melted shortening and beaten egg to milk and add to dry ingredients. Mix well; add flavoring and cocoanut and bake in greased and floured loaf pan in moderate oven at 375° F. thirty-five to forty-five minutes. Sprinkle with powdered sugar or cover with any icing desired.

Makes one seven-inch loaf.

Orange Cup Cakes

4 tablespoons shortening	3 teaspoons Royal Baking
1 cup sugar	Powder
⅔ cup milk	⅛ teaspoon salt
1 egg	1 teaspoon orange extract
2 cups flour	grated rind 1 orange

Cream shortening; add sugar slowly beating well; add milk a little at a time; add beaten egg; sift flour, baking powder and salt together and add to mixture; add flavoring and grated orange rind; mix well. Bake in greased and floured individual cake tins in moderate oven at 380° F. fifteen to twenty minutes. When cool cover with Orange Frosting, page 71.

Makes twelve cup cakes.

Rich Chocolate Cakes

½ cup butter	2 teaspoons Royal Baking Powder
1 cup sugar	¼ teaspoon salt
2 eggs	¼ teaspoon soda
¾ cup milk	1 teaspoon vanilla extract
2 cups flour	2 ½ squares chocolate, melted

Cream butter thoroughly; add sugar a little at a time; separate yolks and whites of eggs. Beat yolks until creamy. Add yolks to creamed butter and sugar; mix thoroughly. Add alternately a little at a time milk and flour, which has been sifted with the baking powder, salt and soda. Then add vanilla and melted chocolate. Fold in stiffly beaten egg whites. Put into greased tins and bake in moderate oven at 375° F. about twenty-five minutes. Cover with Soft Chocolate Icing, page 88.

Makes sixteen cakes.

Strawberry Puffs

1 cup boiling water	⅛ teaspoon salt
½ cup shortening	3 eggs
1 cup flour	2 teaspoons Royal Baking Powder

Heat water and shortening in saucepan until it boils up well; add all at once flour sifted with salt and stir vigorously. Remove from fire as soon as mixed; cool, and mix in unbeaten eggs, one at a time; add baking powder; mix and drop by spoonfuls 1 ½ inches apart on greased tin; shape into circular form with wet spoon. Bake in hot oven at 450° F. and after ten minutes reduce the heat to about 400° F., baking twenty-five minutes or until puffs are light brown and thoroughly cooked. Cut with sharp knife near base to admit following filling:

Strawberry Filling

1 egg white (unbeaten)	½ cup drained strawberry
½ cup granulated or ¾ cup pow-	pulp
dered or confectioner's sugar	¼ teaspoon Royal Baking
	Powder

Place all in bowl and beat with wire egg whip until very stiff. If desired, cover with following icing:

Fresh Strawberry Icing

Crush five large strawberries with a little sugar and a few drops lemon juice, and let stand until juicy; then mix in gradually 1 ½ cups confectioner's sugar; spread on top of each puff.

Makes twenty puffs.

Anise Sticks or Pallilos

2 cups flour	4 tablespoons shortening
1 teaspoon Royal Baking Powder	2 eggs
¼ teaspoon salt	1 or 2 drops anise oil
¾ cup sugar	

Mix and sift dry ingredients. Add shortening and mix in lightly. Add well-beaten eggs and flavoring. Knead lightly on floured board and roll to one-fourth inch thick. Cut into bars, four inches long and one-half inch wide. Place side by side on greased pan; brush tops with melted butter and bake in moderate oven at 325° F. for fifteen minutes.

Makes three dozen.

Shortbreads Royal—Oatmeal Macaroons—on page 64

Maple Nut Cakes

⅓ cup shortening
1 cup light brown sugar
2 eggs
1 teaspoon maple flavoring
   or vanilla extract
½ cup milk

1½ cups flour
¼ teaspoon salt
2 teaspoons Royal Baking Powder
1 cup chopped nuts, preferably
   pecans

Cream shortening; add sugar, egg yolks, flavoring and milk, and beat well; add dry ingredients which have been sifted together, and add chopped nuts; mix in beaten egg whites. Bake in greased and floured individual cake tins in a moderate oven at 375° F. for about twenty-five minutes. Spread tops with the following icing and while still soft sprinkle with chopped nuts.

Maple Icing

½ tablespoon butter
2 tablespoons hot milk

1½ cups confectioner's sugar
½ teaspoon maple flavoring

Add butter to hot milk; add sugar slowly to make paste of the right consistency to spread; add flavoring and spread on cakes.

Makes eight cakes.

Mrs. Gray's Date Dainties

1 pound stoned and chopped
   dates
1 cup chopped nut meats
5 tablespoons flour
¾ cup sugar

2 teaspoons Royal Baking Powder
⅛ teaspoon salt
1 teaspoon vanilla extract
3 eggs

Sift flour and then measure. Sift a second time with the baking powder. Combine all the other ingredients, the eggs unbeaten. Bake in shallow greased pan in moderate oven at 325° F. about forty-five minutes. Cut in squares and sprinkle with powdered sugar.

Makes twenty-five squares (three-quarters inch thick).

Fudge Cake

¼ cup butter
1 cup sugar
1 egg
1 teaspoon vanilla extract
2 squares unsweetened chocolate

½ cup water
1½ cups pastry flour
1½ teaspoons Royal Baking Powder
½ teaspoon salt

Cream butter, add sugar slowly and unbeaten egg. Mix thoroughly and add vanilla and melted chocolate. Then add part of the water and part of the dry ingredients which have been sifted together. Add alternately until all is used. Bake in square greased and lightly floured pan in moderate oven at 400° F. for about thirty minutes. Cool in pan and cover one-half inch thick with following:

Chocolate Fudge Icing

1½ tablespoons butter
2 cups confectioner's
   sugar

1½ squares unsweetened
   chocolate, melted
4-5 tablespoons hot milk

Cream the butter; add sugar gradually, add chocolate and milk, using just enough to make right consistency to spread thickly.

Makes nine two-inch squares.

Madeleines

3 eggs
½ cup sugar
1 cup flour
¼ teaspoon salt

½ teaspoon Royal Baking
   Powder
1 teaspoon vanilla extract
½ cup melted butter

Beat eggs and sugar very light. Fold in flour sifted with salt and baking powder. Add vanilla extract and melted butter. Sprinkle sugar on top and bake in well-greased small individual tins in hot oven at 425° F. twelve minutes. Cover with thin coating of white frosting and decorate with candied fruit.

Makes eighteen.

Nut Bars and Meringues on page 64

Lady Betty Cake

⅔ cup butter	2 teaspoons Royal Baking Powder
1½ cups sugar	1 cup milk
4 eggs	3 squares unsweetened chocolate
1⅔ cups flour	1 cup chopped nuts (walnuts)
¼ teaspoon salt	

Cream butter thoroughly and add sugar, beating continually. Add yolks of eggs; beat well. Sift together flour, salt and baking powder and add nuts. Add this flour mixture and the milk alternately a little at a time to the egg and sugar mixture; mix thoroughly, and add the chocolate which has been melted, just before the last of the flour. Fold in beaten egg whites. Pour into well-greased and floured nine-inch tube pan and bake in moderate oven at 325° F. about one hour and a quarter. Turn out and cool. Cover top and sides with chocolate icing, page 88.

Makes one large loaf about 3½-inches high—baked in nine-inch tube pan.

Orange Sponge Cake

3 eggs	1¼ cups pastry flour
¼ teaspoon cream of tartar	1½ teaspoons Royal Baking Powder
1 cup granulated sugar	
2 teaspoons grated orange rind	¼ teaspoon salt
⅓ cup orange juice	

Separate eggs; beat whites and cream of tartar until stiff and add the yolks one at a time, beating well before addition of each yolk. Add the sugar gradually, still beating with egg beater; remove beater. Add the grated rind and orange juice. Fold in flour, baking powder and salt sifted together. Bake in a moderate oven at 325° F. in two layer cake pans for about eighteen minutes.

Orange Filling

¼ cup sugar	½ cup orange juice
1½ tablespoons flour	1 egg yolk
¼ teaspoon salt	2 teaspoons butter
2 teaspoons grated orange rind	1 teaspoon lemon juice

Put sugar, flour and salt in top of double boiler and mix together thoroughly; add orange rind and orange juice. Add butter and egg yolk and cook until smooth and thick. Remove from fire and add lemon juice. Spread between layers. Ice top and sides of cake with seven-minute icing, page 88. Grate a little orange rind on icing before it cools.

Makes one two-layer cake (eight-inch tins).

Greentree Layer Cake

½ cup shortening	3 teaspoons Royal Baking Powder
1¼ cups sugar	⅔ cup milk
2 eggs	1 teaspoon vanilla extract
2 cups flour	

Cream shortening thoroughly; add sugar slowly, beating until very light and of creamy consistency. Add beaten eggs and part of flour which has been sifted with baking powder. Add milk, a small amount at a time and remainder of the flour. Add flavoring and mix well. Dividing batter evenly pour into four large greased and floured layer cake pans. Spread batter very thin, just to cover the bottom of the pans. Bake in moderate oven at 400° F. for about fifteen minutes. Cool and remove from pans and put together with the following filling and frosting.

Cocoa Almond Filling and Frosting

6 tablespoons butter	½ teaspoon almond extract
3 cups confectioner's sugar	⅓ cup cream
8 tablespoons cocoa	

Cream butter; add sugar and cocoa a little at a time, beating until very light and of creamy consistency. Add flavoring and cream, more if necessary to make the icing soft enough to spread. Spread thickly between layers and put a thin layer on top and sides of cake. With pastry tube (using the tip for a rose border) put icing up and down sides of cake to represent the bark of a tree. Cover top with chopped pistachio nuts. If latter are unavailable use chopped browned almonds.

Makes one four-layer cake (nine-inch tins).

TROPIC AROMA
Recipe on page 69

Tropic Aroma
First Mystery Cake

½ cup shortening	4 teaspoons Royal Baking
1¼ cups sugar	Powder
2 eggs	1 teaspoon nutmeg
2½ cups flour	1 teaspoon cinnamon
¼ teaspoon salt	1 cup milk

Cream shortening; add sugar a little at a time and well-beaten eggs, mixing thoroughly. Sift flour, salt, baking powder and spices together; add a little of the dry ingredients to the first mixture; add milk a small amount at a time and remaining dry ingredients. Bake two-thirds of this batter in two greased and floured layer tins. To remaining third add a tablespoon cocoa, which has been mixed with a tablespoon cold water. Use this for middle layer. Bake layers in moderate oven at 375° F. fifteen to twenty minutes. Put following filling and icing between layers and on top and sides of cake.

3 tablespoons butter	1 teaspoon vanilla extract
3 cups confectioner's sugar	5 tablespoons strong coffee
5 tablespoons cocoa	

Cream butter and add sugar and cocoa very slowly, beating until light and fluffy. Add vanilla and coffee a few drops at a time, making soft enough to spread.

Makes three eight-inch layers.

Mrs. Wetmore's Nut Fudge Cake

2 oz. chocolate	¾ teaspoon Royal Baking Powder
½ cup butter	¼ teaspoon salt
3 eggs	½ cup nuts, pecans or English walnuts chopped or broken
1 cup sugar	
¾ cup flour	
	½ teaspoon vanilla extract

Combine chocolate and butter in saucepan and melt together until blended. Beat eggs with dover beater very light. Add sugar slowly and beat thoroughly. Add the two mixtures (after chocolate and butter has cooled). Beat again. Sift flour, baking powder and salt and add slowly; add vanilla and nuts last. Bake in greased shallow square pan in moderate oven at 350° F. for about thirty-five minutes.

Ice thickly with melted chocolate softened with cream over hot water.

½ cake Maillard's sweet chocolate	1 tablespoon butter
2½ tablespoons cream	few grains salt
	few drops vanilla extract

Makes one seven-inch square cake.

Chocolate Caramel Cake

2 cups dark brown sugar	2½ teaspoons Royal Baking
⅓ cup butter	Powder
2 eggs	2 cups flour
¾ cup milk	¼ teaspoon salt
1 teaspoon vanilla extract	

Mix two tablespoons of the measured sugar and one teaspoon of butter with one tablespoon of the measured milk; boil until it thickens slightly. This is the caramel sauce.

Cream sugar and shortening; add egg yolks and beat; add milk, then caramel sauce. Sift baking powder, flour and salt into batter; add vanilla. Fold in stiffly beaten egg whites. Bake in two greased medium-sized cake pans in moderate oven at 380° F. for twenty minutes.

Icing

2 cups confectioner's sugar	1½ squares unsweetened chocolate, melted
1½ tablespoons butter	4-5 tablespoons hot milk

Cream butter, add sugar slowly, add chocolate and enough milk to make right consistency to spread thickly. Spread between layers and on top of cake.

Makes two nine-inch layers.

Princess Cake

½ cup butter or other shortening	1 cup water
1¼ cups sugar	3 cups pastry flour
½ teaspoon vanilla extract	½ teaspoon salt
½ teaspoon almond or orange extract	4 teaspoons Royal Baking Powder
	5 egg whites

Cream shortening until very light and fluffy; add sugar slowly, beating until light; add flavoring and a little water, then part of flour sifted with salt and baking powder; add remainder of water and remainder of dry ingredients. Fold in beaten egg whites, mixing well, but do not beat. Bake in two greased and floured layer tins in moderate oven at 385° F. for about forty minutes. Remove from pans; cool and spread following filling between layers. Cover top and sides of cake with pink icing.

Caramel Filling and Icing

3 tablespoons butter	3 to 4 tablespoons milk
3½ cups confectioner's sugar	½ cup chopped pecan nuts
4 tablespoons caramel syrup	

Cream butter; add sugar slowly; add syrup and milk a little at a time until of right consistency to spread. Reserve two-thirds this icing for top and sides of cake. Add nuts to remainder and allow to stand about twenty minutes before spreading on cake. Spread thickly between layers.

To plain icing add very little red vegetable coloring to make pale pink.

For Caramel Syrup put two-thirds cup sugar in saucepan and allow to melt, stirring until light golden brown. Add slowly one cup boiling water and boil gently until consistency of syrup.

Makes two layers eight by ten inches.

Lady Baltimore Cake

½ cup butter	¼ teaspoon almond extract
1 cup powdered sugar	¼ teaspoon rose extract
whites of 4 eggs	2 cups pastry flour
½ cup milk	2 teaspoons Royal Baking Powder

Cream butter; add sugar slowly; add unbeaten white of one egg and milk slowly; add flavoring. Add flour sifted with baking powder and fold in three beaten egg whites. Bake in two greased and floured layer tins in moderate oven at 375° F. about 20 minutes.

Filling and Frosting

1½ cups sugar	½ teaspoon vanilla extract
½ cup water	½ cup chopped seeded raisins
whites of 2 eggs	1 cup chopped blanched almonds or pecan nuts
¼ teaspoon Royal Baking Powder	⅓ cup chopped figs

Boil sugar and water without stirring until syrup spins a thread or 238° F. Pour slowly over beaten egg whites, beating continually until thick. Add baking powder and flavoring. Fold in fruits and nuts.

Petite Baltimore Cakes

Bake cake mixture in large cup cake tins. Cut in half crosswise and spread filling and frosting between and on tops and sides of cakes.

Cocoanut Marshmallow Cake

½ cup butter or other shortening	¾ cup milk
1 cup sugar	2 cups pastry flour
3 eggs	3 teaspoons Royal Baking Powder
1 teaspoon lemon juice	¼ teaspoon salt
1 teaspoon vanilla extract	

Reserve two egg whites for icing. Cream shortening; add sugar and yolks of eggs and flavoring; mix well and add half the milk; add half the flour which has been sifted with the baking powder and salt; add remainder of milk then remainder of flour and mix well after each addition. Add white of one egg beaten stiff. Bake in three greased and floured layer cake tins in moderate oven at 400° F. fifteen to twenty minutes. Put together with Cocoanut Marshmallow Filling and Icing, page 88.

Makes three eight-inch layers.

Cake Decoration

Icing

One of three types of icing may be used in cake decoration, namely a "twice cooked" icing, an uncooked icing made with egg white and confectioner's sugar, or the ever popular butter icing. For the beginner the last is easiest to use as it may be worked over many times without injury to the texture and it does not "set" as quickly as either of the others. Recipes for these three are on the next page.

Use of Color

For coloring, the pastes are more desirable than the liquids, since they do not thin a mixture already of the right consistency. Softer shades are obtained when the original icing is cream colored rather than white. This cream color is secured through the use of a yellow fat and egg yolk. Color should be added very carefully, working in minute amounts at the edge of the icing mass at first. If this is not done streaks and spots of intense color will result.

Utensils

Pastry bags of rubber or canvas with inserted metal tips, or metal syringes made for the purpose may be used. It will be found, however, that cones of *heavy* paper, cut as are the metal tips, may be used more advantageously. They are cheaper, easier to use, can be disposed of after using and do very well for the ordinary decoration done in the home. The paper should be heavy in order that the small points made by cutting will be stiff and so make cleancut impressions in the soft material. Heavy manila paper is good, and also the water-proof paper used by many butchers. Glazed white shelf paper, if heavy, may also be used.

Making the Paper Tube

Take a twelve to fifteen-inch square of *heavy* brown or glazed white paper and cut triangle. Take one of the small points in thumb and first finger of left hand with long side of paper away from you and take other end in right hand. Wrap right corner well over left, pulling right point of paper down tight to make a sharp point. When properly made the three points of the triangle will lie together with the largest between the two smaller. Pin at the seam about two inches from the tip, putting point of pin towards point of cone.

Cutting the Tip

Different effects are made by the use of tubes cut in varying ways. Flatten the tube slightly at the tip, keeping the seam on the middle top, with the point toward you. With sharp scissors cut just the tip off and then cut according to the following patterns for the desired decorations. The purpose of each is given under the diagram.

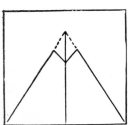

1 *Petals, leaves, butterfly wings*

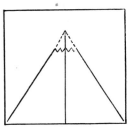

2 *Rosettes, border*

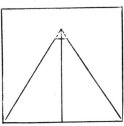

3 *Stems, writing, lines, dots*

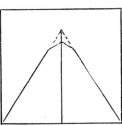

4 *Rose, sweet pea petals*

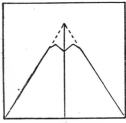

5. *Leaves*

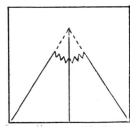

6 *Shells, shell border*

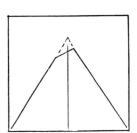

7. *Ribbons*

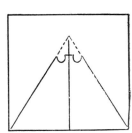

8 *Fancy border*

Use of the Tube

Be sure plain foundation icing is thoroughly set before attempting to ornament a cake.

Have several tubes of each type desired ready before beginning work. Fill not more than half full and fold the sides in towards center, fold the front over them toward the back and lastly fold the back over all three. When using tubes No. 1 and No. 5, turn them so that the point of the V, which was away from you when the tube was cut is at the side. The seam will then be at the side instead of on top, and the sharp point of the tube will point toward the surface to be decorated.

There are two positions for holding the tube, horizontal and vertical. If you wish a leaf to lie flat use the tube in the horizontal position; that is, parallel to the frosted surface of the cake. If you wish the leaf to stand up hold the tube in the vertical position, or at right angles to the working surface.

Always hold the cone with right hand and guide and press with left. Press the icing out gently but hold

Simple Designs with Some Icing Recipes

the tube firmly. When petal or leaf is of the desired size lift the tube quickly, which will break off the icing. If raised gradually a wavering, untidy design will result. For a continuous pattern use the tube in the horizontal position and keep the tip touching the surface all the time. For a shell or leaf border, press out a bit of icing, release the pressure, move the tube but do not raise it, and press again. Continue as far as desired.

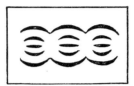

Pressure Released During Moving　　　*Continuous Pressure*

Making the Design

After making and cutting the tube has been mastered, practically all that is needed is practice, beyond a general idea or plan of design. The size of the leaf or petal is determined by the distance of the original cut from the tip of the tube allowing more or less icing to come out as the hole is larger or smaller.

In decorating a medium-sized cake, the design should be kept simple. An ornate cake is never artistic. A border at the edge, a rose, and a few scrolls or sweet peas in the center, are usually sufficient. A large cake may have more. Side decoration should not be attempted until work on the horizontal surface is mastered.

Daisy
Tubes No. 1 and 3

Make a yellow mound for the center. Around it arrange leaf-like petals. May be used on a chocolate cake with white petals and yellow center.

Sweet Pea
Tube No. 1 in two sizes, using the smaller for leaves

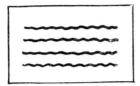

Two small and one large petal with the latter set at right angles to the others, but all flat. Two standing petals on the smaller ones. Leaves should be long and set opposite each other, using tube No. 3 for the stem.

Simple Rose
Tubes No. 4 and 5

Five petals flat and on top of these four petals standing, with one or more in the center of these unless a small yellow center has been made with tube No. 3. For a birthday cake candles may be put in rose centers before icing sets.

Butter Icing

3 cups confectioner's sugar	1 teaspoon vanilla
½ cup butter (part substitute may be used)	1 egg yolk or white
	hot cream, if necessary

Cream the butter; add egg; gradually work in the sugar, beating until very smooth. Add vanilla, and if necessary thin with hot cream. Icing should be stiff enough to have points stand up from the surface when the spoon is quickly lifted but should not break off bluntly. If a pure white icing is desired use an uncolored margarine and the egg white only.

Uncooked Icing

1 unbeaten egg white	1 teaspoon vanilla extract
1½ cups confectioner's sugar	

Put egg white into shallow dish; add sugar gradually, beating with wire whip until of right consistency to spread; add vanilla and spread on cake.

Uncooked Orange Icing

Grated rind of 1 orange	1 egg (well beaten)
1 tablespoon orange juice	1½–2 cups confectioner's sugar
½ teaspoon lemon juice	

To the grated orange rind add orange juice and lemon juice. Let stand fifteen minutes. Strain and add slowly to egg. Stir in confectioner's sugar until of the consistency to spread.

Sufficient to cover seven-inch square cake.

Ornamental or Twice-Cooked Frosting

1½ cups granulated sugar	1 teaspoon flavoring extract
½ cup water	1 teaspoon Royal Baking Powder
2 egg whites	

Boil sugar and water without stirring until syrup spins a thread; add very slowly to beaten egg whites; add flavoring and baking powder and beat until smooth and stiff enough to spread. Put over boiling water, stirring continually until icing grates slightly on bottom of bowl. Spread on cake, saving a small portion of icing to ornament the edge of cake.

Orange Frosting

1 cup sugar	½ tablespoon orange juice or
½ cup water	1 teaspoon orange flavoring
1 egg white	orange rind
1 egg yolk	

Boil sugar and water without stirring to 238° F. or until syrup spins a thread when dropped from spoon. Pour slowly onto egg white which has been beaten until stiff. Beat constantly with egg beater until mixture holds its shape. Then fold in gradually egg yolk, orange rind and juice and spread on cake.

Sufficient to cover top and sides of one round eight-inch layer cake.

Neapolitan Icing

Ice a cake with a thin orange icing; when this is set, add a fairly thick white icing; on top spread a thin layer of melted, unsweetened chocolate.

1 Sift three cups confectioner's sugar into bowl; very carefully separate whites and yolks of four eggs. The whites only are to be used in this icing.

2 Put egg whites in large platter and add one cup sifted sugar, beating with wire whip for about ten minutes.

5 Add one teaspoon rose or almond extract, beating in well with same motion.

6 For foundation frosting place cake on plate a trifle smaller than cake and put this on another larger plate or French plaque. Ice cake, smoothing with spatula. Set aside to cool before decorating.

9 For colored icing, put portions of icing in different bowls and color with a good vegetable color paste or liquid. The daintiest pale shades are the prettiest and require but a very small amount of color.

10 Any icing left may be kept for future use Clean platter with spatula, put icing into small bowl and cover with damp cloth until used.

3 Then add the second cup of sugar with one teaspoon cream of tartar and continue beating.

4 Add the third cup of sugar and continue beating with a long "up and over" motion until icing becomes stiff but smooth and very fluffy.

7 For decorating, beat remaining icing.   The correct stiffness is obtained by long beating.   It must be thick enough to retain shape when pressed through tube.

8 Put icing in pastry tube.   We are using a home-made paper tube here.   For this design cut tip into five points as 5 below or 2 on page 74.   With continuous pressure in this position a very pretty shell border can be made.   To make rosettes similar to 3 below hold upright and lift after pressure.

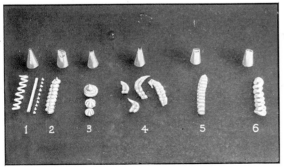

11 Metal tips and the designs they make: 1. Stems, writing, dots (holding tube upright); 2. Ribbon; 3. Rosettes (holding tube upright); 4. Leaves, petals; 5. Shell (holding as in position 8); 6. Border, petals.

12 Cake ornamenting syringe.   Pastry Bag.   Home-made paper pastry tube.

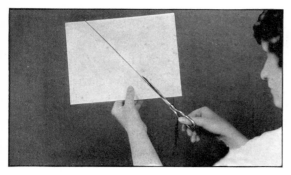

1 Take a twelve- to fifteen-inch piece of heavy brown or glazed white paper and cut triangle.

2 Take one of small points in thumb and first finger of left hand with long side of paper away from you and take other end in right hand.

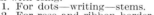

5 Have several paper cones cut and ready for use. Fill with icing.
   1. For dots—writing—stems.
   2. For rose and ribbon border.
   3. For borders and edge work.
   4. For leaves and petals.

6 Now close cone by folding sides of top into center and then center down. It is now ready for work on cake which has been covered with foundation icing.

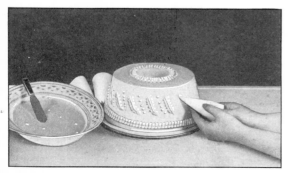

9 Showing position for side work. The plain tip, 1, is used for the dots and tip 4 for leaf design.

10 Decorating top of cake. Note position of hands and tube.

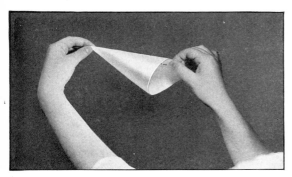

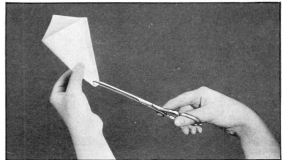

3 Wrap right corner well over left, pulling right point of paper down tight to make a sharp point. Fasten with pin about three inches from top.

4 Flatten tube at tip and with sharp scissors cut point straight off. Then cut tip for any desired decoration.

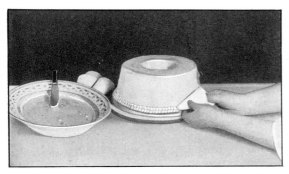

7 Showing position for edge work. Always hold with right hand and guide and press with left hand. The tip, 2, is used for this ribbon border.

8 Showing position of tube and hands for drop work.

11 Set cake in protected place such as an open cool oven for icing to dry off.

12 Finished cake. A wreath of fresh flowers or smilax or asparagus ferns arranged around cake is appropriate and often used.

President's Fruit Cake

1 cup shortening	2 teaspoons melted chocolate
1 cup sugar	½ lb citron
6 eggs	½ cup grape juice
½ glass grape jelly	2½ lbs. raisins
2 teaspoons cinnamon	½ lb. crystallized cherries
¼ teaspoon nutmeg	½ lb. crystallized pineapple
¼ teaspoon allspice	⅛ lb. orange paste (Turkish paste
2½ cups flour	will do)
1 teaspoon Royal Baking	½ lb. blanched and ground almonds
Powder	½ lb. pecans

(Cut fruit in small pieces and soak overnight in grape juice.)
Cream shortening and half the sugar.

Beat yolks of eggs very light with remaining sugar—combine the two; add jelly and spices. Sift baking powder with half the flour and add alternately with stiffly beaten egg whites, then chocolate. Sift remaining half of flour over fruit and add to batter; put in nuts last. Place in loaf cake pans, the sides and bottoms of which are lined with fitted greased heavy brown paper. Steam slowly for six hours. Place in slow oven at 250° F. and allow to dry out for an hour. This recipe may be doubled exactly if a larger cake is desired. (See page 98 for special instructions).

Makes three cakes in loaf pans 5 by 9 inches.

Mrs. Wilson's Bride's Cake

1 cup shortening	¼ teaspoon salt
2 cups sugar	1¼ cups sweet milk
4½ cups flour	8 egg whites
5 teaspoons Royal Baking	1 teaspoon almond extract
Powder	1½ teaspoons vanilla extract

Cream shortening and sugar together well. Sift flour, baking powder and salt together five times; add alternately a little at a time with the milk and beat thoroughly. Add egg whites which have been beaten stiff and flavoring last. Bake in moderate oven at 325° F. until perfectly firm to the touch or about one hour and ten minutes. When cool cover with the following:

Frosting

4 egg whites	1 teaspoon lemon juice
2¼ cups granulated sugar	½ teaspoon Royal Baking
1 cup water	Powder

Cook two cups sugar and water until it forms a fairly thick drop from tip of spoon at 222° F.

Beat egg whites with wire whisk. Gradually beat in the one-fourth cup granulated sugar. Beat in one-third of the cooked syrup. Continue to cook the syrup until it threads very fine at 230° F. Add another third of the syrup to the egg whites and beat in very thoroughly. Cook remaining third of syrup until two drops fall at once from the spoon at 250° F. Beat it into egg whites. Add baking powder and lemon juice. Cook over hot water, folding it over, but not beating, until thick enough to pile high without spreading and sinking. Cool. When ready to use on cake, fold it over carefully until smooth and creamy.

Makes 1½ quarts, sufficient for two Bride's Cakes.

Jack Frost Triangles

½ cup shortening	1¾ cups pastry flour
¾ cup granulated sugar	¼ teaspoon salt
⅔ cup milk	3 teaspoons Royal Baking
1 teaspoon almond or vanilla	Powder
extract	2 egg whites

Cream shortening until light and creamy, add sugar slowly, add milk and flavoring very slowly, beating continually. Stir in flour sifted with dry ingredients; fold in beaten egg whites. Pour into greased Golden Rod pans and bake in moderate oven at 375° F. ten to fifteen minutes. Cool and cover the triangles with pistachio icing, then drop over this a little white icing to represent icicles.

Makes twenty-four.

Devil's Food Cake

⅔ cup butter	¼ teaspoon salt
1½ cups sugar	3 teaspoons Royal Baking Powder
3 eggs	1 teaspoon vanilla extract
1 cup milk	3 oz. unsweetened chocolate,
2½ cups flour	melted

Cream butter thoroughly; add sugar a little at a time. Separate yolks and white of eggs. Beat yolks until creamy. Add yolks to creamed butter and sugar; mix thoroughly. Add milk and the flour which has been sifted with the baking powder and salt, alternately—a little at a time. Then add vanilla and melted chocolate. Fold in stiffly-beaten egg whites. Put into three greased and floured cake tins and bake twenty-five to thirty minutes in moderate oven at 350° F.

Icing and Filling

½ tablespoon butter	3½ cups confectioner's sugar
5 tablespoons milk	1 teaspoon vanilla extract
3 oz. unsweetened chocolate	

Heat butter, milk and chocolate in top of double boiler; add sugar slowly, beating continually; add flavoring and beat until creamy; if necessary add more milk and spread thickly between layers and on top and sides of cake.

Makes three eight-inch layers.

Mrs. Wetmore's One Egg Cakes with Minute Fudge Frosting

¼ cup butter	1 egg
⅔ cup sugar	2 teaspoons Royal Baking Powder
½ cup rich milk	1 teaspoon vanilla extract
1½ cup pastry flour	⅛ teaspoon salt

Cream the butter well; add the sugar gradually, mixing thoroughly. Add the egg unbeaten and stir well. Measure the pastry flour after sifting, then sift again with Royal Baking Powder and salt; add to first mixture alternately with milk stirring—not beating—add vanilla and half fill very small greased cake tins. Put into a moderate oven, temperature at 375° F. and bake for about eight minutes. Do not bake too brown, as the softness and daintiness of these cakes depend upon baking.

Minute Fudge Frosting

½ cup cocoa	1 cup sugar
¼ cup milk or thin cream	1 teaspoon vanilla extract
4 tablespoons butter	⅛ teaspoon salt

Combine all ingredients, except vanilla, and place over low flame (or with asbestos lid) and let it melt slowly stirring gently from bottom until it comes to a boil. Then let it boil without stirring for one minute exactly. Remove from fire. Beat immediately until it begins to thicken. Add the vanilla and frost the little cakes either on top or upside down. This frosting will harden after being put onto the cakes and be shiny. If it hardens too fast while icing small cakes moisten with hot water.

Makes thirty small cakes.

Mrs. Gray's Nut Tea Cakes

⅓ cup butter	1 cup nut meats, cut in small
1 cup sugar	pieces
½ cup milk	whites 3 eggs
2 cups pastry flour	⅛ teaspoon salt
2 teaspoons Royal Baking	1 teaspoon vanilla extract
Powder	

Cream butter; add sugar, add flour sifted with baking powder alternately with the milk. Add any nut meats (walnuts are usually used) dusted with one tablespoon of flour, and lastly fold in the slightly beaten egg whites to which the salt has been added. Add vanilla. Bake in well oiled small tins in moderate oven at 375° F. about fifteen minutes. When cool cover with Mocha Icing and roll in finely chopped nuts.

Makes thirty small cakes.

Chocolate Layer Cake

½ cup butter
1 cup sugar
2 eggs
1 teaspoon vanilla extract
1 cup milk
2½ cups pastry flour
3 teaspoons Royal Baking Powder
¼ teaspoon salt

Cream butter; add sugar, a little at a time, beating until very light; add beaten yolks and flavoring; add part of the flour, which has been sifted with salt and baking powder; add part of milk and remaining flour and milk, a little at a time until all is added. Fold in egg whites, beaten stiff. Bake in three greased and floured layer cake pans in moderate oven at 375° F. twenty minutes. Spread filling thickly between layers and cover top and sides with icing.

Old-Fashioned Chocolate Filling

2 ½ squares (2 ½ oz.) chocolate
3 tablespoons cream
¾ cup confectioner's or powdered sugar
1 tablespoon cornstarch
1 egg yolk
⅛ teaspoon salt
1 teaspoon vanilla extract

Melt chocolate in double boiler; add cream and mix in sugar slowly; add cornstarch mixed with a little cold water; add egg yolk and cook, stirring constantly until smooth and thick. Remove from fire; add salt and vanilla.

Chocolate Icing

2½ squares (2 ½ oz.) chocolate
1 tablespoon butter
1 unbeaten egg white
2 cups confectioner's sugar
2-3 tablespoons thin cream

Melt chocolate with butter; put egg white into shallow dish; add sugar slowly, beating until light and smooth; add chocolate and sufficient cream to make right consistency to spread.

Makes one three-layer cake (eight-inch tins).

Frosty Fruit Cake

⅓ cup butter
1 cup sugar
2 eggs
1 teaspoon vanilla extract
1 cup milk
2 cups flour
3 teaspoons Royal Baking Powder
¼ teaspoon salt

Cream butter thoroughly; add sugar a little at a time, beating well; add yolks of eggs and vanilla; beat thoroughly; add milk alternately with dry ingredients which have been sifted together; mix well but do not beat. Mix in beaten egg whites. Bake in three greased and lightly floured layer cake pans in moderate oven at 375° F. for twenty minutes. Put layers together—after they have cooled with following

DEVIL'S FOOD CAKE
Recipe on page 76

Fruit Filling and Frosting

2 ½ cups granulated sugar
¾ cup boiling water
1 teaspoon Royal Baking Powder
2 egg whites
1 teaspoon lemon juice
1 cup mixed figs, cherries and pineapple, cut fine

Boil sugar, water and baking powder without stirring until syrup spins a thread at 238° F. Beat egg whites until dry; add syrup gradually, beating constantly until right consistency to spread; add flavoring and cool. Add fruit to one-third this icing and spread thickly between layers. Cover top and sides of cake with remaining plain icing. Decorate top with nuts if desired. Some of the fruits may be omitted as the choice is a matter of taste.

Makes three layers baked in eight-inch pans—sixteen servings.

Mocha Tart

4 eggs
1 tablespoon mocha essence or
2 tablespoons cold strong coffee
few grains salt
1 cup sugar
1 cup flour
1 teaspoon Royal Baking Powder

Separate eggs; beat yolks until light; add mocha, salt and sugar gradually, beating continually; add flour and baking powder sifted together; fold in stiffly beaten whites; mix thoroughly without beating. Spread in two well-buttered layer pans; bake in slow oven ten to fifteen minutes, starting at 300° F. increasing temperature last half of baking to 375° F. Whip one-half pint cream; add one-third cup powdered sugar and 1 tablespoon mocha essence. Spread between layers and on top of cake. Sprinkle top with chopped, browned almonds.

Makes one two-layer cake (nine-inch pans).

Afternoon Tea Cakes
Baked in frilled paper cases

1 egg	1 cup pastry flour
¾ cup sugar	1 teaspoon Royal Baking Powder
2 tablespoons butter, melted	½ teaspoon salt
1 ½ squares chocolate, melted	⅔ cup milk

Separate egg. Beat yolk well; add sugar slowly, continuing to beat. Add melted butter and chocolate. Sift flour, baking powder and salt and add alternately with milk. Fold in stiffly beaten egg white.

Partly fill the paper cups, set each in muffin tin and bake in moderate oven at 345° F. for fifteen minutes. Decorate with nuts or cherries in white frosting.

Very nice for parties and when used for children's party, decorate each cake with a teaspoon of confectioner's sugar frosting, the sugar being moistened with hot milk, teaspoon butter, flavored and pushed out of spoon with forefinger to make a little mound. On each mound stand an animal cracker.

Makes thirty-two very small cakes.

Mrs. Moody's Wonder Cake

½ cup butter	2 teaspoons Royal Baking Powder
1 ½ cups powdered sugar	1 teaspoon vanilla extract
½ cup milk	6 egg whites
2 cups pastry flour	

Cream butter with powdered sugar; add alternately a little at a time, milk and pastry flour which has been sifted with baking powder. Add vanilla and fold in beaten egg whites. Bake in three buttered layer tins in moderate oven at 325° F. twenty minutes. Increase to 350° F. last half of baking.

Fruit Filling and Frosting

1 ½ cups granulated sugar	½ cup shaved pecans
½ cup water	⅓ cup chopped figs
3 egg whites, beaten	⅓ teaspoon vanilla extract
⅓ cup muscatel raisins (cut in pieces)	

Boil sugar with water until syrup spins a thread at 238° F. Add slowly to egg whites, beating continually until cool. Add raisins, pecans, figs and vanilla. Spread between layers and on top and sides of cake.

Makes three eight-inch layers.

PRESIDENT'S FRUIT CAKE
Recipe on page 76

Easter Bunny Cake

4 eggs	¼ teaspoon salt
1 ½ cups granulated sugar	1 cup boiling water
2 cup pastry flour	1 teaspoon lemon extract
2 teaspoons Royal Baking Powder	

Beat eggs until very light. Beat in the sugar a little at a time and then the flour which has been sifted with salt and baking powder. Add the boiling water, a small amount at a time, and the flavoring. Put into ungreased large size angel cake tin. Bake in a slow oven for about one hour, starting at 250° F. and increasing to 350° F.

When cake is cold, frost as follows:

1 ½ cups confectioner's sugar	2 teaspoons melted butter
2 tablespoons milk	green vegetable coloring
½ teaspoon almond extract	

Moisten sugar with milk until proper consistency to spread. Add flavoring and spread on top and sides of cake, saving a small amount of icing. Add melted butter to this and a very little green coloring, to make a delicate shade. Decorate rim of cake with this green icing, allowing it to drip over edge to resemble grass. While frosting is soft, make bunnies with large, fresh marshmallows which are pinched with thumb and finger at one end for nose and at other for tail. Dip toothpick in melted chocolate and make dots for eyes. Large ears are cut from white writing paper. Arrange a row of these bunnies around edge of cake.

Makes one eight-inch loaf.

Orange Blossoms

6 tablespoons shortening	1 ¼ cups pastry flour
⅔ cup fine granulated sugar	2 tablespoons cornstarch
½ teaspoon almond extract	2 ½ teaspoons Royal Baking Powder
½ cup cold water	2 egg whites

Cream shortening well. Add sugar slowly, beating until light and fluffy. Add almond extract. Sift flour, cornstarch and baking powder together three or four times and add alternately a little at a time with the water. Whip egg whites until light but not dry; fold in, mixing well with batter. Bake in greased very small tins in moderate oven at 365° F. for fifteen minutes. Remove from tins, cool and cover with following

Orange Icing

3 tablespoons butter	grated rind and pulp of ½ small
2 cups confectioner's sugar	orange
1 tablespoon orange juice	1 egg white, beaten
	candied orange peel

Cream butter until soft and very light. Add sugar very slowly, beating well between each addition. Add orange juice, rind and pulp of orange. Mix well and fold in egg white. Spread on cakes and place small piece of candied peel on each top.

Makes from twenty-eight to thirty small cakes.

Lady Goldenglow

½ cup shortening	¼ teaspoon salt
1 ½ cups sugar	4 teaspoons Royal Baking Powder
grated rind of ½ orange	1 cup milk
1 egg and 1 yolk	1 ½ squares (1 ½ oz.) chocolate,
2 ½ cups flour	melted

Cream shortening, add sugar and orange rind. Add beaten egg yolks. Sift together flour, baking powder and salt and add alternately with the milk; lastly fold in one beaten egg white. Divide batter into two parts. To one part add the melted chocolate. Put by tablespoonfuls alternating dark and light batter, into three greased and floured layer cake pans. Bake in moderate oven at 375° F. twenty minutes.

Orange Chocolate Icing

3 tablespoons melted butter	grated rind of ½ orange and pulp
3 cups confectioner's sugar	of 1 orange
(powdered will not give as	1 egg white
good results)	3 squares (3 ounces) chocolate
2 tablespoons orange juice	

Put butter, sugar, orange juice and rind into bowl. Cut pulp from orange, removing skin and seeds, and add. Beat all together until smooth. Fold in beaten egg white. Spread this icing on layer used for top of cake. While icing is soft sprinkle with unsweetened chocolate shaved in fine pieces with sharp knife (use one-half square). To remaining icing add 2 ½ squares (2 ½ ounces) unsweetened chocolate which has been melted. Spread this thickly between layers and on sides of cake.

Makes one three-layer cake (nine-inch pans).

MRS. WILSON'S BRIDE CAKE
Recipe on page 76

Merry-Go-Round Cake
Children's Birthday Cake

½ cup butter	2 cups pastry flour
1 cup sugar	2 teaspoons Royal Baking Powder
1 egg	½ teaspoon vanilla extract
⅔ cup milk	

Cream butter. Add sugar slowly and beaten egg. Beat batter until very light and fluffy. Sift flour and baking powder together and add a little at a time alternately with the milk. Add flavor. Put in small round greased tin or iron spider. Bake in moderate oven at 350° F. for about forty-five minutes. Turn out of pan and cool.

Icing

1 tablespoon butter	2 cups confectioner's sugar
3 tablespoons hot milk or cream	½ teaspoon vanilla extract

Add butter to hot milk and add slowly to sugar until right consistency to spread. Add vanilla. Ice top and sides of cake. While icing is still soft stand animal crackers, which have been decorated with daintily colored icing, and pink candles alternately around the edge of cake.

Makes one loaf (seven-inch tin).

Strawberry Pie

Use standard recipe for pastry, page 81. Bake in very hot oven at 500° F. twelve to fifteen minutes.

For glazed crust, brush edges after baking with boiling hot syrup (two tablespoons sugar and one tablespoon water) and return to oven for one or two minutes until syrup hardens. Fill baked crust with fresh selected strawberries and cover with following syrup:

Bring to a boil one-half cup sugar, one-half cup strawberries, and two cups boiling water; strain; add one tablespoon cornstarch which has been mixed with a little cold water. Cook over hot fire for a minute or two, stirring constantly; remove from fire and beat hard; return to slow fire and cook very gently until thick. Pour while hot over strawberries. Serve either hot or cold.

Mrs. Scott's Baked Apple Buns

1 ½ cups whole wheat flour	½ cup milk
½ cup white flour	2 tablespoons melted butter
4 teaspoons Royal Baking Powder	1 pint chopped cooking apples
½ teaspoon salt	1 cup brown sugar
3 tablespoons shortening	1 teaspoon cinnamon

Sift dry ingredients into bowl; add shortening and rub in lightly. Add milk to make a smooth dough; roll out in oblong sheet one-fourth inch thick; brush with butter and cover with the apples. Sprinkle with three-fourths cup sugar and dust with cinnamon. Rub edges with cold water and roll same as jelly roll. Cut into 1 ½ inch pieces and place in bake dish liberally brushed with butter and bottom covered with the one-fourth cup of sugar. Place in moderate oven at 325° F. and bake twenty minutes; then put an asbestos pad under pan and bake twenty-five to thirty minutes longer at 350° F. Sprinkle top with sugar and remove from pan at once.

This makes an exceptionally good luncheon or supper dessert. Makes six buns.

Individual Strawberry Shortcakes

2 cups flour	4 tablespoons shortening
3 teaspoons Royal Baking Powder	1 egg
1 tablespoon sugar	½ cup water
½ teaspoon salt	1 quart strawberries
	whipped cream

Sift together flour, baking powder, sugar and salt; add shortening and mix thoroughly with steel fork; add water to beaten egg and add slowly to make a soft dough. Roll or pat out with hands on floured board to about one-half inch thick. Cut with very large biscuit cutter, dipped in flour, or half fill large greased muffin rings which have been placed on baking pan. Bake in hot oven at 475° F. ten to twelve minutes. Split while hot; butter and fill with crushed and slightly sweetened strawberries. Put on the tops and cover with strawberries and sweetened whipped cream. Garnish with whole berries.

Makes six shortcakes.

Peach Dumplings

1 ½ cups flour	5 tablespoons shortening
3 teaspoons Royal Baking Powder	½ cup milk
½ teaspoon salt	6 peaches
	6 tablespoons sugar

Sift together flour, baking powder and salt; rub shortening in lightly; add just enough milk to make soft dough. Roll out to one-eighth inch thick on slightly floured board; divide into six equal parts; lay on each piece a peach which has been pared; sprinkle with sugar; moisten edges of dough and fold up around the peach, pressing tightly together. Place in greased baking pan; sprinkle with sugar and put a piece of butter on top of each dumpling. Bake about forty minutes in moderate oven at 400° F. Serve with hard sauce.

Makes six dumplings.

Standard Recipe for Plain Pastry

1 cup pastry flour	1/3 cup shortening
1/4 teaspoon salt	2-3 tablespoons cold water

Sift flour and salt into bowl; add half shortening and rub in lightly with finger tips or mix in with a steel fork; add water slowly and just enough to roll out. Roll out very thin on slightly floured board; dot paste with small pieces of remaining shortening; fold upper and lower edges to center; fold sides to center; fold sides to center again; chill. Roll out very thin and use for lower crust of pie or for tarts. Bake in very hot oven at 500° F. for about five minutes. If baked with filling, continue at lower temperature until pie is baked.

Makes one crust for nine-inch pie.

If inexperienced in pastry making better results are obtained by adding baking powder.

When baking powder is used, sift one-half teaspoon Royal Baking Powder in with flour and salt.

Flour. Use pastry flour, or if bread flour take two tablespoons less, and add one tablespoon cornstarch.

Shortening. Lard or half butter and half lard, or any vegetable shortening may be used.

For a rich pastry see page 82.

Common Causes of Failure. Too much water, too slow an oven and too much handling. Pastry should be very lightly and quickly handled. When possible, chill paste before using for pie.

Hot Water Pastry

1 1/2 cups flour	1/2 teaspoon salt
1/2 teaspoon Royal Baking Powder	1/2 cup solid shortening
	1/4 cup boiling water

Sift dry ingredients and rub in fat with a fork until well mixed but not too fine. Add enough water to make a stiff paste. Roll out on a well floured board as desired.

Spicy Fruit Pie

3/4 cup seeded raisins	2 tablespoons vinegar
2 cups finely cut citron or preserved watermelon rind	Grated rind 1/2 lemon
3/4 cup brown sugar	Grated rind 1/2 orange
2 tablespoons butter	1/2 teaspoon cinnamon
2 cups hot water	1/2 teaspoon grated nutmeg

Place the above ingredients in saucepan and cook slowly for twelve minutes; thicken with one tablespoon cornstarch mixed with cold water; cool and pour into pie plate lined with rich pastry. Cover with strips of paste and bake in hot oven at 450° F. until brown.

Makes one small pie.

Butterscotch Pie

3 egg yolks	1/4 teaspoon salt
1 cup brown sugar	3 tablespoons butter
3 1/2 tablespoons cornstarch	1 teaspoon vanilla extract
2 cups milk	

Beat egg yolks with sugar; mix cornstarch with a little water to make a smooth paste; add to first mixture, then add milk and salt. Cook in double boiler until thick. Remove from fire; add butter and vanilla. Cool; add beaten whites of eggs, or reserve for a meringue. Pour into a baked crust. If meringue is used, spread on top and return to oven to brown. Otherwise spread top with sweetened whipped cream.

Makes one small pie.

Lemon Meringue Pie

Filling

2 cups water	3 egg yolks
4 tablespoons cornstarch	4–6 tablespoons lemon juice
2 tablespoons flour	2 teaspoons grated lemon rind
1 cup sugar	1 teaspoon salt

Put water on to boil. Mix cornstarch, flour and sugar with one-half cup cold water until smooth; mix in egg yolks, slightly beaten; add slowly to boiling water. Cook five minutes, stirring constantly; remove from fire; add lemon juice, rind and salt. Pour into a baked crust.

Meringue

3 egg whites	1 teaspoon Royal Baking Powder
3 tablespoons sugar	

Beat egg whites; add sugar slowly and baking powder, beating between each addition; spread thickly on top of pie. Bake in moderate oven at 325° F. for ten minutes or until light brown.

Makes one nine-inch pie.

Custard Pie

3 eggs	2 cups milk
3/4 cup sugar	1 teaspoon vanilla extract
1 teaspoon salt	

Beat eggs slightly; add sugar, salt and scalded milk slowly. Line pie plate with plain or rich paste and pour in custard. Bake in moderate oven at 325° F. twenty-five to thirty minutes. The custard is baked when a knife put in center comes out dry.

Cocoanut Pie

Follow recipe for Custard Pie, using only two eggs and adding one cup fresh grated cocoanut.

Pumpkin Pie

2 cups stewed pumpkin	1/2 teaspoon salt
2 cups rich milk or cream	1/2 teaspoon ginger
1 cup sugar	2 teaspoons cinnamon
2 eggs	1/2 teaspoon allspice

Strain pumpkin and mix with milk, sugar, beaten eggs, salt and spices and beat two minutes. Pour into pie plate which has been lined with pastry. Place in hot oven at 475° F. for fifteen minutes, then reduce the heat and bake forty-five minutes in moderate oven at 400° F. Long, slow cooking brings out the flavor of the pumpkin.

Makes one nine-inch pie.

Lemon Puff Pie

1/2 cup sugar	3 egg whites
3 egg yolks	1/2 cup sugar
3 tablespoons hot water	1/8 teaspoon salt
Juice and rind of 1 lemon	1/2 teaspoon Royal Baking Powder

Combine first three ingredients and cook over boiling water until thick. Add lemon juice and rind. Beat egg whites stiff and dry and gradually beat in the sugar and continue beating until thick. Add baking powder. Combine first mixture with meringue, mixing thoroughly. Put into a baked pastry shell and bake in a moderate oven at 350° F. until set and slightly browned.

Makes one small pie.

Chocolate Pie

3/4 cup sugar	1/4 teaspoon salt
1/3 cup cornstarch	1 teaspoon vanilla
1/2 cup cocoa	1 quart milk

Mix sugar, cornstarch, cocoa and salt thoroughly together. Add a little of the measured milk to cocoa mixture and add to remainder of milk, cooking over hot water until smooth and thick. Add vanilla and pour into a baked crust. Chill and just before serving spread thickly with sweetened whipped cream. 2 1/2 oz. chocolate may be used in place of cocoa.

Makes sufficient for two pies.

1 Put one cup of butter (one-half pound) in a bowl; add cold water and work or "wash" out the salt with fingers.

2 Scrape butter from sides of bowl and press out all water. Put the butter on a clean cloth to dry and put one side.

5 Turn out on slightly floured board and knead very lightly until smooth.

6 Then cover with a towel and let stand for about five minutes.

9 Fold first upper and then lower edge of paste into center.

10 Now fold first one side and then other into center.

3 Sift four cups sifted pastry flour, one teaspoon salt and one teaspoon Royal Baking Powder together into bowl. Add one-third cup shortening; cut in lightly with steel fork.

4 As soon as mixed add ice water slowly to make stiff dough and of right consistency to roll out.

7 Flour rolling pin just enough to keep from sticking; roll out paste very lightly, starting from center and rolling out to edge each way to about one-half inch thick.

8 Take butter (entire cupful) from cloth and put on paste in small pieces.

11 Roll lightly away from center until about one-fourth inch thick. Fold ends towards center again, making three layers as before. Roll and let stand five minutes.

12 Roll out again and fold ends toward center; repeat this three times and then put away to chill thoroughly until ready to use for pies or tarts. This paste will keep perfectly for several days if it is kept covered in cold place.

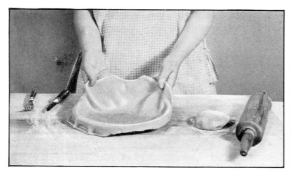

1 APPLE PIE—Two Crusts—Take one-fourth of the paste shown on preceding page and cut into halves; roll one-half very thin on very slightly floured board; place loosely over pie plate, bringing paste well over edge of plate. Press paste around edge and trim.

2 Sprinkle a little flour and sugar, mixed together, over paste. Fill with sliced and cored apples, about one quart; sprinkle with one-third cup sugar, one-half teaspoon salt, a little cinnamon or nutmeg, and dot with pieces of butter.

1 LEMON MERINGUE PIE—One Crust—Line pie plate loosely with paste; prick bottom with fork; trim off edges and bake in very hot oven at 500° F. about 10 minutes.

2 Fill with cooled lemon filling and using tablespoon cover thickly with meringue, recipe on page 81. Put in moderate oven at 325° F. for about ten minutes or until a delicate brown.

1 "LATTICE TOP" BERRY PIE—Use one-fourth of the paste on preceding page and roll half of it very thin. Line pie plate as above; sprinkle lightly with flour and sugar, mixed, to prevent juice from soaking in crust.

2 Fill with berries which have been picked over, washed and drained; sprinkle with flour and little salt; cover with two-thirds cup sugar and dot with small pieces of butter.

3 Roll out other half of paste and place loosely over pie, pressing edges tightly together with fork.

4 Cut a few slits in top; trim off edges of paste and pie is ready to bake in hot oven at 450° F. for 40 to 45 minutes. Reduce temperature to 375° F. last part of baking. Save any ends of paste left over and use for tarts.

3 Lemon Meringue Pie can be served either slightly warm or cold, whichever way is preferred.

For Tarts and Patty Shells, roll paste thin; cut into even pieces; cover reverse of muffin tins; prick; trim and bake in very hot oven at 500° F. about 12 minutes or until light brown.

3 Cut remaining paste into long narrow strips and place them evenly across pie; press paste together where they join edge. Lay other strips across top to form a lattice. Trim and bake in hot oven at 450° F. for about 25 minutes.

4 Blueberry, cranberry, peach, cherry, and rhubarb pies and tarts can be made in exactly the same way.

Menus for Special Occasions

Afternoon Teas

WHEN serving hot tea very thin slices of lemon and cream should always appear on the tea table, and, if desired, cloves, thin half-slices of oranges, and candied cherries may also be served.

Coffee or chocolate with whipped cream are usually included at formal teas, and in warm weather these drinks iced and fruit punches take the place of hot tea, coffee, and chocolate.

Sandwiches should be very thin and dainty, cut with fancy cutters or rolled, and may be made with any filling that is not too strongly flavored. On page 93 will be found directions for making sandwiches with a few suggestions for fillings.

It is perhaps unnecessary to add that salted nuts, olives, ices, and sweets complete the formal tea table.

Rolled Watercress Sandwiches
Brown Bread and Butter Sandwiches
Pimento and Cheese Sandwiches
Tea   Chocolate
Shortbreads Royal
Swedish Sand Tarts   Rochester Ginger Snaps
Crystallized Ginger
Mints

Cucumber Sandwiches
Nut and Cheese Rolled Sandwiches
Lobster Paste Toast Sandwiches
Pâté de Foie Gras Toast Sandwiches
Tea   Olives   Salted Nuts   Coffee
Pineapple Ice
Madeleines   Anise Sticks

Sardine Paste Toast Sandwiches
Lettuce Sandwiches
Asparagus Mayonnaise Sandwiches
Tea   Salted Nuts   Coffee
Crystallized Fruit
Almond Macaroons   Rochester Molasses Wafers
Orange Blossoms

Avocado Sandwiches
Brown Bread Cheese Pineapple Sandwiches
Ginger Cheese Graham Bread Sandwiches
Tea   Salted Almonds   Chocolate
Strawberry Mousse
Meringues   Brownies   Jack Frost Triangles

Buffet Suppers

The following menus may be used for buffet suppers, bridge teas or suppers, and Sunday night suppers. They are all planned to serve from sideboard or central table to small tables where guests are seated.

Hot dishes and hot beverages are kept hot in electric grills and urns on sideboard, from which guests usually serve themselves.

Mushroom Patties
Finger Rolls   Celery Curls
Chicken in Aspic
Coffee   Tea
Olives   Salted Nuts
Crème aux Marrons

Oysters and Mushrooms à la Poulette
Olives   Stuffed Celery
Tomato Aspic Salad
Cheese Biscuits
Demi Tasse

Assorted Hors d'oeuvres
Lobster Thermidor
Lettuce Sandwiches   Pâté de Foie Gras Sandwiches
Coffee   Ginger Ale
Pineapple Jelly
Lady Fingers

Ham Roulade   Julienne Potatoes
Grapefruit Mayonnaise Salad
Hot Buttered Rolls   Salted Almonds
Coffee

Baked Ham
Frozen Tomato Salad
Scalloped Oysters
Tea Biscuits   Celery
Coffee
Peach Ice Cream
Nuns Cake   Angel Food

Caviar Canapés
Anchovy Canapés
Curried Chicken on Toast
Coffee   Saratoga Chips   Tea
Hot Biscuits

Fresh Fruit Cup
Salad Parisienne
Cold Sliced Chicken
Stuffed Celery   Olives
Parker House Rolls
Raspberry Ice   Vanilla Mousse
Demi Tasse

Evening Suppers

That Will Interest the 16-Year-Old

Every young girl is anxious to give a party that is different and to be assured that her boy and girl friends are going to have as fine a time at her home as at any other. The kinds of cake or sandwiches or other dishes that the boys like will always be the ones decided upon. The selections below are apt to be most popular with them.

Many of the dishes suggested can be prepared on the electric grill, and their preparation on the table with the help of the guests contributes to the success of the party.

Broiled American Cheese and Bacon on Toast
Doughnuts   Nut Fudge Cake
Cider   Coffee

Waffles   Chicken Hash
        Coffee

Chopped Ham and Horseradish Sandwiches
Cucumber, Onion and Parsley Sandwiches
        Anchovy Appetizers
Coffee   Ginger Ale
Stuffed Celery   Olives   Pin-Money Pickles
        Devil's Food Cake
        Vanilla Mousse

        Oysters in Cream on Toast
Celery   Hot Rolls   Stuffed Olives
        Coffee   Salted Nuts
    Cocoanut Marshmallow Layer Cake
        Chocolate Ice Cream

    Swiss Cheese Sandwiches Broiled
        Waldorf Salad
Coffee   Salted Nuts
        Crêpes Suzette

Picnic Luncheons or Suppers

Picnics may be held on the beach, in the woods, and along the open road, and even on one's own porch or lawn, just so long as you are in the out-of-doors with good friends and good food. The food may be ever so simple, including only a sandwich or two, or it may be very elaborate with a great variety of dishes. Generally the lunch or supper must be carried some distance. It is, therefore, quite necessary to pack the food carefully, if possible in containers that can be thrown away.

If you have a fitted hamper you can safely carry the most delectable foods, and if not paraffin paper containers will carry salads, etc., nicely.

Sandwiches should be wrapped singly or in sets of two in waxed paper, and then all put in larger box.

Hot Soup or *Hot Coffee* or *Cold Drinks* may be carried in Thermos bottles or Thermos jugs without change of temperature.

Ice Cream is carried in the freezer or packed in ice and salt.

Chicken may be cut into convenient pieces and each wrapped in waxed paper, making knives and forks unnecessary.

Biscuits taken from the oven just before leaving the house can be split, buttered and filled with sliced ham, and if wrapped separately in waxed paper, will keep warm for some time.

Paper plates, paper cups, and paper spoons are convenient and suitable, and paper napkins in generous supply are quite necessary.

A picnic is hardly a picnic unless some cooking is included in the program. The following is a list of foods that are easily prepared over a picnic fire, or for the more elaborate picnic, on an improvised stove.

Steamed Clams	Roasted Corn
Baked Clams	Baked Potatoes
Boiled Lobster	Fried Bacon
Broiled Lobster	Fried Eggs
Broiled Steaks	Baking Powder Biscuits
Broiled Chops	Flapjacks
Broiled Chicken	Coffee
Steamed Corn	Soup

Picnic Menus

Hot Biscuits with Ham Sandwiches
Sardine Sandwiches
Egg, Onion, Parsley Sandwiches
Whole Tomatoes   Stuffed Eggs
        Pin-Money Pickles
        Hot Coffee
        Chocolate Layer Cake

Fried Chicken   Stuffed Olives   Pickles
        Potted Ham Sandwiches
    Cream Cheese and Pimento Sandwiches
        Hot Coffee
        Strawberry Ice Cream
    Cup Cakes with Chocolate Icing

    Bacon and American Cheese Sandwiches
        Sliced Chicken Sandwiches
Hot Coffee   Olives
        Cold Boiled Lobster
        with Mayonnaise
        Buttered Rolls
Pears   Peaches   Bananas
        Cocoanut Layer Cake
        Brownies

    Steamed Clams   Clam Broth
Broiled Steak   Steamed Corn
            Hot Rolls
    Mustard Pickles   Olives
        Lobster or Chicken Salad
        Peach Ice Cream
    Betty's Feather Sponge Cake
        Iced Coffee

Uncooked Icing I

1 unbeaten egg white   1 teaspoon vanilla extract
1½ cups confectioner's sugar

Put egg white into shallow dish; add sugar gradually, beating with wire whip until of right consistency to spread; add vanilla and spread on cake.

Uncooked Icing II

1½ cups confectioner's sugar   ½ tablespoon butter
2 tablespoons hot milk   ½ teaspoon vanilla extract

Add butter to hot milk; add sugar slowly to make right consistency to spread; add vanilla. Spread on cake.

PINK ICING. Add one tablespoon strawberry or other fruit juices in place of one tablespoon milk.

YELLOW ICING. Add one teaspoon egg yolk and flavor with orange rind and one teaspoon lemon juice.

PISTACHIO ICING. Color with very little green vegetable paste and flavor with one-half teaspoon pistachio or almond extract instead of vanilla.

Seven Minute Frosting

1 unbeaten egg white   3 tablespoons cold water
⅞ cup granulated sugar   ½ teaspoon Royal Baking Powder

Place all of the ingredients except the baking powder in the top of a double boiler. Place over boiling water and beat with beater for seven minutes. Add one-half teaspoon flavoring and baking powder; beat and spread on cake.

MARSHMALLOW SEVEN MINUTE FROSTING. Add eight marshmallows, cut fine, after frosting becomes thick. Beat until the marshmallows melt.

CHOCOLATE SEVEN MINUTE FROSTING. Add to above 1½ ounces melted unsweetened chocolate two minutes before taking from fire and beat four minutes longer.

COFFEE SEVEN MINUTE FROSTING. Add three tablespoons cold boiled coffee in place of water or simply add one teaspoon coffee extract to Seven Minute Frosting.

Chocolate Icing

whites of 2 eggs   1 teaspoon vanilla extract
2 cups confectioner's sugar   4 ounces unsweetened chocolate
1½ tablespoons milk   1 teaspoon butter

Beat whites until stiff; add sugar slowly; beating well; add milk, vanilla and chocolate which has been melted with butter; mix until smooth. Spread on cake.

Soft Chocolate Icing

Melt six ounces (six squares) unsweetened chocolate in double boiler. Add three cups confectioner's sugar, stirring constantly. Add slowly three-fourths cup cream. Add three tablespoons boiling water and spread while hot on cake which has cooled.

Sea Foam Frosting

½ cup light brown sugar   ¼ teaspoon cream of tartar
1 cup granulated sugar   whites of 2 eggs
¼ cup water   ⅛ teaspoon salt
2 tablespoons strong coffee

Boil sugar, water, coffee and cream of tartar without stirring until syrup spins a thread at 248° F. Pour hot syrup very slowly over beaten egg whites, beating continually about five minutes or until thick. Add salt; whip again and spread very thickly on cake.

Divinity Frosting

2 cups sugar   ⅛ teaspoon salt
¼ cup white corn syrup   1 teaspoon vanilla extract
⅔ cup hot water   1 teaspoon Royal Baking
2 egg whites   Powder

Mix sugar, syrup and water; cook to 238° F. or until syrup forms a soft ball when dropped in cold water. Pour very slowly over the well beaten whites of eggs and continue beating until mixture becomes creamy and will just hold its shape; beat in flavoring, salt and baking powder.

Cocoa Icing

1 cup confectioner's sugar   1 teaspoon vanilla extract
4 tablespoons cocoa   1 tablespoon cream
1 egg white   2 teaspoons melted butter

Add sugar and cocoa slowly to beaten egg white. Then add vanilla, melted butter and cream to make soft enough to spread on cake.

Maple Frosting

1 cup maple syrup   whites of 2 eggs

Boil syrup without stirring until it spins a thread; add slowly to stiffly beaten egg whites; beat with wire whip, preferably on platter, until stiff enough to spread.

Mock Maple Icing

½ cup brown sugar   1 tablespoon butter
½ cup granulated sugar   1 teaspoon maple flavoring or
½ cup cream   vanilla extract

Put the sugar and cream into sauce pan and stir gently until it comes to a boil. Then boil for exactly fifteen minutes. Remove from fire, add butter and flavoring and beat with silver fork until it becomes creamy enough to put on cake. If frosting becomes too stiff for use, thin with a teaspoon or two of cream.

Sufficient for twenty-two small cakes.

Cocoanut Marshmallow Frosting

1½ cups granulated sugar   whites of 2 eggs
½ cup water   1 cup fresh grated cocoanut
6 marshmallows—large size   2 teaspoons lemon juice

Boil sugar and water until syrup spins a thread at 238° F. Add marshmallows which have been cut into very small pieces, but do not stir into syrup. Pour very slowly on stiffly beaten whites of eggs and beat until smooth. Add lemon juice. Spread between layers. Sprinkle with cocoanut and small pieces of marshmallows. Cover top of cake with icing, sprinkle thickly with cocoanut and decorate top with pieces of marshmallow.

Sufficient for three layers.

Butterscotch Icing
(*Without Sugar*)

2 cups light syrup   ½ cup milk
½ cup butter

Boil syrup, butter and milk together until it forms a soft ball when tested in cold water. Cool slightly without stirring and pour while warm on cake. Chopped nuts may be added while icing is still soft.

Cocoanut Frosting

Add one cup fresh grated cocoanut to boiled frosting and sprinkle with cocoanut after spreading on cake.

Chocolate Filling

¾ cup milk	½ cup sugar
1½ squares (1½ oz.) unsweet-	1 egg
ened chocolate	¼ teaspoon salt
¼ cup flour	½ teaspoon vanilla **extract**
1 tablespoon butter	

Scald milk with chocolate and thicken with flour mixed with one-fourth cup cold milk; add butter. Beat sugar, egg and salt together and add. Cook over hot water until smooth and thick. Add vanilla and spread on cake.

Coffee Butter Icing

2 cups confectioner's sugar	2 tablespoons soft butter
4 tablespoons cold *strong* coffee	

Mix sugar and coffee together and beat until smooth. Beat in the soft but unmelted butter. Add more coffee if necessary to make icing good consistency to spread.

Apricot Icing

1 cup apricot pulp	1 tablespoon lemon juice
3 cups confectioner's sugar	1 tablespoon butter

Cook dried apricots without sweetening in a small amount of water; drain, and while hot rub them through a fine hair sieve; when cold add three cups confectioner's sugar to apricot pulp, mixing until smooth; add softened butter and lemon juice.

Sufficient for filling and icing one two-layer cake.

Fresh Strawberry Icing

Crush ten strawberries with a little sugar and few drops lemon juice and let stand until juicy; mix in gradually three cups of confectioner's sugar. Spread between layers and on top of cake.

Nut and Fruit Filling

2 cups granulated sugar	¼ cup chopped nuts
⅔ cup boiling water	1 cup mixed figs, raisins, citron,
whites of 2 eggs	cherries and pineapple, cut fine

Boil sugar and water without stirring until syrup spins a thread at 238° F. Beat whites until dry; add syrup gradually, beating constantly; when cool add nuts and fruit. Spread between layers of cake.

Strawberry Filling

1 egg white (unbeaten)	½ cup granulated or ¾ cup
½ cup drained strawberry	powdered or confectioner's
pulp	sugar

Place all in bowl and beat with wire egg whip until very stiff.

Jelly Meringue

white of 1 egg	½ cup currant or other jelly

Put egg white and jelly together into bowl and beat with egg beater or wire whip until stiff. Spread between layers or on top of cake.

Pineapple Cream Filling

1 cup shredded pineapple	½ pint cream

Drain some of the juice from the pineapple and spread thickly over lower part of cake. Place a layer of the cream which has been whipped and slightly sweetened thickly over the pineapple.

Vanilla Cream Filling

½ cup sugar	1 cup scalded milk
2 tablespoons cornstarch	2 teaspoons butter
⅛ teaspoon salt	½ teaspoon vanilla extract
2 eggs	

Mix sugar, cornstarch, salt and beaten eggs; pour on gradually scalded milk; add butter; cook in double boiler until thick and smooth, stirring constantly; add flavoring.

Coffee Cream Filling

Follow directions for Vanilla Cream Filling, adding one tablespoon very finely ground coffee to scalded milk. Strain before adding to dry ingredients.

Chocolate Cream Filling

1 cup sugar	2 cups scalded milk
⅓ cup flour	2 teaspoons butter
¼ teaspoon salt	1½ squares unsweetened chocolate
2 eggs	1 teaspoon vanilla extract

Mix dry ingredients. Add eggs slightly beaten. Add the scalded milk slowly and cook in double boiler until thick and smooth. Add chocolate which has been melted, butter and flavoring.

Lemon Filling

3 tablespoons cornstarch	2 egg yolks
1 cup sugar	2 tablespoons butter
¾ cup water	grated rind of one lemon
¼ cup lemon juice	½ teaspoon lemon extract

Mix cornstarch and sugar (except 2 tablespoons sugar) in top of double boiler. Add water slowly and cook over hot water until thick, stirring to prevent lumping. Add lemon juice. Add egg yolks mixed with the 2 tablespoons sugar, cook three minutes longer and beat until smooth. Add butter, grated lemon rind and lemon extract.

Other Filling and Frosting Recipes

Cottage Pudding

1 cup pastry flour
½ cup sugar
⅛ teaspoon salt
2 teaspoons Royal Baking Powder
½ cup milk
1 egg, beaten
2 tablespoons melted butter or other shortening

Sift dry ingredients; add milk, egg and butter; beat well and bake in greased shallow or ring pan in hot oven at 425° F. about fifteen minutes. Serve hot with chocolate, lemon or other fruit sauce.

Steamed Chocolate Pudding

¼ cup butter
¾ cup sugar
2 eggs
2½ oz. (2½ sq.) unsweetened chocolate, melted
1 cup milk
2 cups pastry flour
4 teaspoons Royal Baking Powder
⅛ teaspoon salt
1 teaspoon vanilla extract

Cream butter; add sugar gradually. Add egg yolks and beat well. Add melted and cooled chocolate. Sift together dry ingredients and add alternately with the milk. Fold in stiffly beaten whites of eggs. Add vanilla extract. Pour into large well-greased mould or several small moulds, cover tightly and steam 2 hours. Serve with sweetened whipped cream or sauce.

Steamed Fig Pudding

¼ cup shortening
1 cup sugar
1 egg
1 cup milk
2 cups flour
4 teaspoons Royal Baking Powder
⅛ teaspoon salt
½ teaspoon vanilla or lemon extract
1½ cups chopped figs

Cream shortening; add sugar slowly and beaten egg; add milk; mix well; add flour, baking powder and salt, which have been sifted together; add flavoring and figs. Pour into greased pudding mould; cover tightly and steam for two hours. Serve with foamy sauce.

Christmas Plum Pudding

2 cups ground suet
2 cups bread crumbs
2 cups flour
2 teaspoons Royal Baking Powder
2 cups sugar
2 cups seeded raisins
2 cups currants
1 cup finely cut citron
1 cup finely cut fig
1 tablespoon finely cut orange peel
1 tablespoon finely cut lemon peel
1 teaspoon ground cinnamon
1 teaspoon ground ginger
¼ teaspoon ground cloves
¼ teaspoon ground nutmeg
¼ teaspoon ground mace
1 teaspoon salt
1 cup water
1 cup grape or other fruit juice

Mix thoroughly all dry ingredients and add fruit; stir in water and fruit juice and mix thoroughly. Add more water if necessary to make stiff dough. Fill greased moulds two-thirds full, and steam five or six hours. This pudding should be prepared and cooked a week or more before used. Before serving steam one hour and serve with hard, lemon or foamy sauce.

Snowballs

4 tablespoons butter
few drops lemon juice
½ cup sugar
⅔ cup milk
1½ cups pastry flour
¼ teaspoon salt
3 teaspoons Royal Baking Powder
2 egg whites
½ teaspoon vanilla extract

Cream butter, adding few drops lemon juice to make butter light colored. Gradually add the sugar. Sift flour, baking powder and salt together. Add alternately with the milk to creamed butter and sugar. Add vanilla and fold in stiffly beaten egg whites. Half fill small greased cups. Cover tightly and steam about thirty minutes.

Serve hot with lemon or any fruit sauce.

Makes six to eight.

Hard Sauce

⅓ cup butter
1 cup powdered or confectioner's sugar
½ teaspoon flavoring extract

Beat butter until very soft; add sugar slowly, beating until light and creamy. Add flavoring and beat thoroughly for ten minutes. Grate nutmeg and an orange peel over top.

Lemon or Orange Sauce

1 cup water
2 tablespoons lemon or orange juice
2 tablespoons sugar
1 teaspoon cornstarch

Boil water, sugar and cornstarch mixed with little cold water. Boil five minutes and add fruit juice and one tablespoon caramel if dark color is desired.

Foamy Sauce

6 tablespoons butter
1 cup powdered sugar
3 eggs
1 teaspoon vanilla extract
2 tablespoons boiling water

Cream butter; add sugar slowly, beating continually; beat egg yolks until thick and add gradually; beat well; add stiffly beaten egg whites, flavoring and water. Before serving heat over boiling water five minutes, stirring constantly.

Chocolate Sauce

1 ounce unsweetened chocolate
2 tablespoons butter
½ cup boiling water
½ cup sugar
½ teaspoon vanilla extract

Melt chocolate in top of double boiler. Add butter and when mixed pour water on slowly, stirring constantly, then add sugar. Bring to boiling point and boil five minutes without stirring; add vanilla and few grains salt and serve hot.

Ice Cream Sauce

1 egg
few grains salt
3 tablespoons sugar
½ cup heavy cream
1½ teaspoons vanilla extract

Separate egg.

Beat white of egg and salt until stiff; gradually beat in the sugar. Beat cream until stiff. Beat yolk of egg, add to the beaten white of egg, and beat all together well. Fold in beaten cream, and add vanilla extract. Maple, coffee or other flavoring may be used.

Fruit Sauce

⅓ cup butter
1 cup powdered sugar
white of 1 egg
1 cup fresh strawberries, raspberries or canned fruit drained from syrup

Cream butter; add sugar gradually; add egg white beaten until stiff and beat well; add slowly fruit which has been carefully prepared and mashed. Beat until creamy.

Caramel Sauce

2 cups granulated sugar
5 cups boiling water

Melt sugar in saucepan and heat, stirring constantly until light golden brown; add boiling water. Cook three minutes.

Custard Sauce

2 egg yolks
¼ cup sugar
⅛ teaspoon salt
2 cups milk, scalded
½ teaspoon flavoring extract

Beat egg yolks slightly, add sugar and salt. Add milk slowly, stirring constantly. Cook in double boiler, stirring until thick enough to coat spoon. Chill and add flavoring. If curdled, beat with egg beater until smooth. Flavor with lemon, orange, vanilla or bitter almond extract.

Cocoa Cream Roll

½ cup powdered sugar	⅛ teaspoon salt
2½ tablespoons cocoa	3 eggs
3 tablespoons flour	1 cup cream, whipped
1 teaspoon Royal Baking Powder	

Sift together sugar, cocoa, flour, baking powder and salt. Beat yolks until light and thick and gradually add sifted ingredients. Fold in egg whites beaten stiff. Put into greased shallow pan; spread very thin, about one-fourth inch, and bake in moderate oven at 350° F. for fifteen minutes. Spread with cream, sweetened and flavored. Roll up as for jelly roll. Sprinkle with powdered sugar. Cut into 1½-inch pieces to serve.

Banana Cake

1 cup pastry flour	¼ teaspoon salt
2 teaspoons Royal Baking Powder	¾ cup milk
	1 egg
2 tablespoons sugar	4 bananas

Sift together dry ingredients; add milk and beaten egg; mix well. Peel and scrape bananas; cut in halves lengthwise, then across. Pour batter into greased shallow pan, place bananas on top and sprinkle with sugar and lemon juice. Bake in moderate oven at 375° F. fifteen minutes. Serve with Jelly Sauce.

Apple Dumpling

3 sour apples	¼ teaspoon salt
1 cup sugar	1 beaten egg
¾ cup flour	½ cup milk
1 teaspoon Royal Baking Powder	1 tablespoon melted butter

Core, pare and chop apples and mix with sugar. Have ready a batter made by sifting flour, baking powder and salt together; add beaten egg and milk to make a drop batter. Stir in melted butter. Mix apples with batter until every piece is coated, then fill greased baking cups and bake in a moderate oven at 375° F. about thirty minutes, or until firm and brown on top. Serve hot with cream or hard or lemon sauce.

Orange Cream Meringue

¼ cup shortening	1 cup flour
½ cup sugar	2 teaspoons Royal Baking Powder
4 eggs	
1 teaspoon vanilla extract	¼ cup milk

Cream shortening and sugar well; add egg yolks which have been beaten, and vanilla. Sift flour and baking powder; add to first mixture alternately with milk. Spread in two shallow pans; cover batter with egg whites beaten stiff mixed with three-fourths cup sugar; sprinkle one-fourth cup chopped almonds over all. Bake in moderate oven at 325° F. about thirty minutes. Spread the following between layers:

Orange Cream Filling

¼ cup sugar	1 cup scalded milk
1 tablespoon cornstarch	½ teaspoon vanilla extract
2 yolks of eggs	grated rind of 1 orange

Mix cornstarch and sugar; add eggs, slightly beaten, and pour gradually on the hot milk. Cook in double boiler, stirring constantly until thickened. Cool and flavor with vanilla and orange rind.

Old-Fashioned Strawberry Shortcake

Use shortcake recipe on page 80. Divide dough in half. Shape half to fit greased deep pie plate. Spread with butter. Shape other half and lay on top. Bake in hot oven at 425° F. for about thirty minutes. Increase heat to 450° F. last part of baking. Put very ripe crushed and sweetened strawberries between and on top of layers. Serve slightly warm.

Royal Pineapple Dessert

1 cup sugar	½ teaspoon salt
½ cup water	2 teaspoons Royal Baking Powder
3 eggs	⅛ cup cold water
1 cup flour	1 teaspoon vanilla extract

Make a sponge cake as for Orange Sponge, page 68, and bake in ungreased deep tube pan in moderate oven at 350° F. about forty-five minutes.

Ice top of cake only with plain white frosting and mark icing in wedges. Allow cake to cool. When cold slice off entire top about one inch deep. Put between layers the following filling:

1 cup shredded pineapple	½ pint cream

Drain some of the juice from the pineapple and spread thickly over lower part of cake. Place a layer of the cream, which has been whipped and slightly sweetened, thickly over the pineapple. Put on top layer; place a rosette of whipped cream about the size of a silver dollar in the center of each wedge and drop a spoonful of shredded pineapple in the center of the whipped cream rosette.

Cocoa Cream Cake

⅓ cup shortening	1¾ cups flour
1 cup sugar	3 teaspoons Royal Baking Powder
2 eggs	
½ cup milk	¼ teaspoon salt
1 teaspoon vanilla extract	

Cream shortening until very light; add sugar slowly, beaten eggs, one-half of the milk, flavoring and mix thoroughly; add half the flour, sifted with the salt and baking powder; add remainder of milk and flour, mixing well after each addition. Bake in two greased and floured layer tins in moderate oven at 380° F. for about twenty minutes. Cool and spread between layers and on top of cake the following:

Cocoa Cream Filling

6 tablespoons cocoa	1 teaspoon vanilla extract
½ cup powdered sugar	1½ cups cream
⅛ teaspoon salt	

Mix the cocoa, sugar and salt with a little hot water until well blended. Cool and add flavoring and cream; whip until stiff enough to spread.

Mahogany Cake

½ cup milk	½ cup cocoa

Cook until thick and smooth and set aside to cool.

½ cup butter	¾ teaspoon soda
1½ cups sugar	2 teaspoons Royal Baking Powder
3 eggs	⅔ cup sweet milk
2 cups pastry flour	1 teaspoon vanilla extract

Cream butter and sugar together well. Add beaten yolks of eggs. Sift together flour, soda and baking powder and add alternately with the milk to the first mixture. Add the chocolate mixture and vanilla extract and mix well. Fold in stiffly beaten whites of eggs. Bake in two well-greased nine-inch layer cake tins, in a moderate oven at 350° F. for about 30 minutes. Cool and spread the following frosting between layers and on top and sides of cake.

Fudge Frosting

2 cups sugar	½ cup milk
2 tablespoons corn syrup	½ teaspoon Royal Baking Powder
3 sq. (3 oz.) unsweetened chocolate	2 tablespoons butter
	1 teaspoon vanilla extract

Put sugar, corn syrup, chocolate and milk into saucepan. Stir until sugar is dissolved. Then cook to 232° F. or until syrup forms a very soft ball when tested in cold water. Stir occasionally while cooking to prevent burning. Remove from fire, and add Royal Baking Powder and butter. Cool to lukewarm. Add vanilla extract and beat until creamy and right consistency to spread.

Lobster Salad

Cut cold boiled lobster into small pieces. Marinate with very little French dressing; put on lettuce leaves; cover with mayonnaise and garnish with olives, hard-boiled eggs cut into pieces, and capers. Arrange lobster claws around lobster on edge of dish.

Fish Salad

2 cups shredded lettuce	1 teaspoon onion juice
1 can tuna fish, or 1½ pounds	½ cup mayonnaise
any cold boiled fish	1 cup finely cut celery
½ cup French dressing	1 teaspoon chopped parsley

Line dish with lettuce; place fish in center; pour over French dressing to which onion juice has been added and cover with celery; put mayonnaise on top. Sprinkle with chopped parsley.

Royal Fruit Salad

Cut skin from two grapefruit and three oranges. Cut out the sections, removing any seeds. Drain and add to three slices pineapple cut in small pieces and one pound Malaga grapes which have been peeled, cut lengthwise and seeds removed. Chill. Serve on lettuce leaves with cream dressing.

Stuffed Eggs Royal Salad

Shell three hard-cooked eggs. Cut in halves crosswise. Remove yolks and mix with four tablespoons each chopped ham and mayonnaise dressing, and little cayenne to taste. Fill egg whites with mixture and place on slices of tomato arranged on bed of water cress which has been washed and chilled. Garnish with mayonnaise and strips of pimento.

Chicken Salad

1 quart cold boiled chicken	⅛ teaspoon pepper
cut into cubes	2 hard boiled eggs
1 pint finely cut celery	2 cups mayonnaise dressing
1 teaspoon salt	6 olives

Mix chicken, which should be very tender, with celery, seasoning and one egg cut into small pieces; marinate with little French dressing, and let stand in cold place one hour. Serve on lettuce leaves and spread mayonnaise over top. Garnish with olives and remaining egg cut into slices. Sprinkle with paprika.

Salad Parisienne

Drain and season with salt freshly cooked string beans cut into short thin strips. Peel and dice cucumbers and season with salt. Cut cold boiled new potatoes into small slices and sprinkle with a little chopped chives. Mix each separately with French dressing. Place large unbroken piece of cold boiled salmon in center of salad plate and the potatoes, cucumbers and beans in alternate piles on lettuce leaves arranged around the fish. Garnish the salmon with mayonnaise dressing.

Artichoke Salad

Boil artichokes until very soft, usually about one hour. They should be softer than when served whole. With spoon scrape off leaves and put with the heart of artichoke, discarding all of the "choke," through sieve or mash with fork. Add for each artichoke, one tablespoon, each finely chopped, celery and parsley, one chopped hard-boiled egg, salt, cayenne, paprika and pepper to taste. Mix well with French dressing to hold together. Put mixture in mould or for individual serving in cup; chill. Just before serving, turn out on lettuce leaves. Cover each mould with mayonnaise and garnish with strips of pimento.

Other Simple Combinations for Salads

1. Halves of canned pears, drained from syrup, hollows filled with seasoned cream cheese balls, garnished with strips of pimento with mayonnaise dressing.

2. Combinations of cooked cauliflower, beans, beets, carrots, peas, spinach and asparagus tips on lettuce with French or mayonnaise dressing.

3. Crab meat with green pepper in tomato aspic with mayonnaise dressing.

4. Apples cut in cubes, garnished with green pepper strips on lettuce with mayonnaise dressing.

5. Sections of grapefruit and avocado arranged alternately on romaine with French dressing.

French Dressing

Put two tablespoons lemon juice or vinegar, one-half teaspoon salt, one-eighth teaspoon pepper, one-half teaspoon powdered sugar and few grains cayenne pepper into bowl; add six tablespoons oil, beating constantly. Add one-half teaspoon Worcestershire sauce if desired. Serve very cold.

Mayonnaise

1 egg yolk	⅛ teaspoon cayenne
¼ teaspoon dry mustard	1 cup salad oil
½ teaspoon salt	2 tablespoons vinegar or
¼ teaspoon powdered sugar	lemon juice

Put egg yolk in bowl; add seasoning, mix well, using rotary egg beater; add oil slowly at first. Thin with vinegar; continue adding oil and vinegar until all is used.

Boiled Salad Dressing

½ tablespoon salt	½ cup vinegar
1½ tablespoons sugar	2 eggs
1 teaspoon mustard	¾ cup milk
½ tablespoon flour	1 tablespoon butter or other
Few grains cayenne	shortening

Mix dry ingredients in top of double boiler; add vinegar and beaten egg yolks and mix; add milk and butter. Cook over hot water until thick and smooth. Take from fire and add beaten egg whites. Cool and serve.

Hollandaise Sauce

½ cup butter	Salt
2 beaten egg yolks	Cayenne
1 tablespoon lemon juice	½ cup boiling water

Cream butter; add gradually, stirring well, egg yolks, lemon juice, salt and cayenne, and boiling water slowly. Stir over boiling water till thick as boiled custard. Serve immediately.

Other Dressings

RUSSIAN DRESSING: Mix with one cup mayonnaise two tablespoons Chili sauce and one can pimentos chopped fine. If desired a dash of grated cheese may be added.

CREAM DRESSING for fruit salads: Just before serving mix one-third to one-half cup stiffly whipped cream with one-half cup mayonnaise.

THOUSAND ISLAND DRESSING: With one cup mayonnaise mix four tablespoons chopped pimentos, two tablespoons chopped olives and one-quarter teaspoon salt; or simply add six tablespoons chopped stuffed olives.

HORSERADISH DRESSING for cold meats, meat salads and sandwiches: With one cup mayonnaise mix thoroughly four tablespoons grated horseradish, well drained, one-half tablespoon onion juice or finely chopped onion.

ROQUEFORT DRESSING: To one cup French dressing add four tablespoons Roquefort cheese which has been mashed with a fork.

Sandwiches

To secure the best results, use bread that is of fine texture and moist. The day before, or several hours before bread is to be used, cut off entire crust before slicing; wrap in damp napkin and keep in ice box until ready to use.

You will find this loaf will now cut into very thin slices and will be much easier to make into sandwiches.

An economical way is to slice the loaf lengthwise and then spread with desired filling and put together before cutting into various shapes.

These suggestions are for white bread sandwiches. The steamed brown bread can be used without previously putting in ice box.

Mexican Sandwich Filling

1 cup tomatoes—as little juice as possible   1 cup shredded beef
½ can Spanish pimentos   ¼ pound American cheese   Seasoning

Break beef into small pieces; put into saucepan and cook without extra fat until brown. Add pimentos, cut small, and tomatoes and stew until well blended. Cut cheese into fine pieces and add, stirring until melted and well mixed. Season with salt, pepper and paprika to taste. Chill and spread between slices of bread or toast.

Rolled Sandwiches

The day, or several hours before sandwiches are to be served, cut entire crust from loaf of bread. Wrap in damp napkin and put in refrigerator.

Slice loaf lengthwise very thin. Spread lightly with butter and then with mixture desired. Cream cheese, seasoned and mixed with finely chopped nuts or chopped olives or chopped pimentos or the avocado mixture below are excellent fillings for this type of sandwich.

Roll each long slice up very carefully and wrap again in damp napkin. Just before serving slice in thin rounds. These sandwiches are very attractive for tea or reception.

Broiled Swiss Cheese Sandwiches

Cut thin slices of white bread. Do not remove crusts. Butter each slice. Put a slice of Swiss cheese on each. Sprinkle with paprika and salt, cover with another buttered slice of bread. Put on broiler over pan and pour a few drops of milk over each. Broil until browned slightly and cheese has melted. Serve hot.

Other Delicious Sandwich Fillings

1. To boned sardines add little mayonnaise, lemon juice, Worcestershire, salt and cayenne to taste. Mix with fork and spread on lightly buttered bread.

2. To chopped hard-cooked eggs add a few drops onion juice and mayonnaise. Spread thickly between slices of bread which have been spread lightly with butter and anchovy paste.

3. To chopped or potted ham add mayonnaise.

4. To chopped cucumbers, add little chopped onion and parsley and mayonnaise to hold mixture together.

5. Spread very thin small squares of bread thickly with mayonnaise. Drain canned asparagus tips and roll one in each square of bread. Roll from corner to corner so that tip shows. Sprinkle the tip with paprika.

6. Put cold boiled lobster or shrimp through the food chopper. Mix to a paste with mayonnaise. Spread between thin pieces of toasted or plain bread.

7. Put cold baked ham through food chopper, add horseradish dressing to make a paste.

Salted Almonds

Blanch almonds by putting in boiling water and boiling one or two minutes. Drain and skins will come off easily. Dry well and put in hot olive oil or butter in large iron frying pan and stir continually until a light brown. If preferred almonds can be browned in oil or butter in shallow pan in oven. Drain well on unglazed paper and sprinkle with salt.

Stuffed Celery

Mix with each cream cheese, one tablespoon cream, dash cayenne and one teaspoon Worcestershire sauce and one-half teaspoon salt. Or add to the first three ingredients one-third cup chopped salted almonds. Or add to first five ingredients two chopped Spanish pimentos. Fill celery stalks which have been prepared with any of these fillings and sprinkle with paprika.

Stuffed Eggs for Picnics

Put eggs in cold water—allow to come to a boil and boil for twenty to thirty minutes. Pour off water and cool in shells. Remove shell and cut each egg across horizontally. Remove yolks and put in bowl. Add salt, pepper and a little cayenne, small amount of chopped ham, and mayonnaise to make smooth paste. Return mixture to egg whites, put together and wrap each carefully in waxed paper for a picnic lunch.

Avocado Appetizers

Cut small rounds of bread, and toast both sides. Spread each with the following mixture:

Peel avocados and put through ricer or mash up with fork. Add one tablespoon onion juice, one tablespoon lemon juice, paprika, salt and cayenne to taste. Mix with just enough mayonnaise to hold together. Spread on toast just before serving and press a round of plain or stuffed olives in center of each. If avocado pit is placed on top of mixture, it will keep green until ready to use.

This also makes delicious sandwiches spread between thin slices of either white or graham bread.

Caviar Appetizers

Toast both sides, small rounds of bread. Spread each with highly seasoned mayonnaise. In center put Russian caviar, add dash of cayenne and a few drops each of onion juice and lemon juice. Surround the caviar with chopped yolk of hard boiled egg and sprinkle with paprika. Press small round of olive in center of caviar.

Caviar canapés are made in same way, only the above is put on larger rounds of fresh untoasted bread.

Sardine Appetizers

Make a paste of sardines, softened butter, few drops Worcestershire sauce, a little pepper, cayenne, salt and lemon juice. Spread on thin rounds of toasted bread. Cut stuffed olives in rings and put one in center of each appetizer.

Anchovy Appetizers

On small toasted rounds of bread, spread a thin coating of mayonnaise dressing. Add thin slice of tomato. In center of each put small amount mayonnaise and a plain anchovy or anchovy stuffed with caper. Arrange around the anchovy narrow strips of plain olive.

1 BISCUITS—Cut Royal biscuit dough with small cutter or cover of 4-ounce Royal tin. If you take three-quarters of the standard recipe it will make eight biscuits on the grill and sufficient for two people.

2 Heat deep pan about five minutes.

5 Biscuits will be well raised and browned in 12 minutes.

6 Turn over each biscuit and brush with butter or other shortening, milk or cream and put back to brown about five minutes.

2 You will find that a pitcher is most convenient for holding the batter. Serve immediately on hot plate with butter, maple syrup, or honey.

1 GRIDDLE CAKES—While griddle is heating about five minutes, make recipe, page 29. Pour small amount for each cake on ungreased griddle.

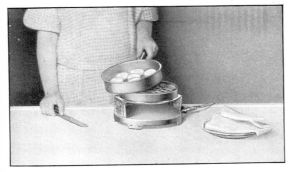

3 When very hot, place biscuits in deep ungreased pan and allow to remain on top of wires three minutes.

4 Next place pan under wires, being sure to leave off top deflector.

7 Any standard grill will bake from seven to nine biscuits in about 20 minutes and baking can be done on your dining-room table if you wish.

1 WAFFLES—While making up waffle batter, page 29, heat grill about 10 minutes. Put about four tablespoons batter in center hot, ungreased iron. Close and bake about two minutes.

2 As soon as bubbles appear, turn and brown other side.

3 When nicely and evenly browned place on hot plate. Do not pile more than four and serve immediately with butter and maple syrup or cinnamon and powdered sugar.

A very interesting and unusual service in very old pewter with hand-made silver from Georg Jensen, of West Fifty-seventh Street, New York, furnishes this luncheon table. White lilacs and delicate blue iris against the soft grey of the pewter pitcher make a lovely centerpiece on the rare old pine table with its time-softened finish.

Lobster Cocktail
Consommé Royal
Educators
Filet of Sole, Marguery
Broiled Guinea Hen
Wild Rice   String Beans
Salted Almonds   Currant Jelly   Celery
Cloverleaf Rolls
Romaine, French Dressing
Coupe Sicilienne
Nut Bars   Madeleines
Rose and Peppermint Leaves
Demi Tasse

Here the silver for all courses is placed on the table, but it is also correct to show only three forks at the left of the plate and place the cocktail or oyster fork at the extreme right next to the soup spoon. The spoon for the last course next to the plate, may be omitted and placed with the dessert.

It is a matter of personal preference as to the folding of the napkin, but if monogrammed it should be folded so the monogram is in the center. It is, however, generally in better taste to have as few folds as is necessary. The napkin is placed either at the extreme left of the cover or on the service plate.

As butter is not served with the formal luncheon or dinner, butter plates and butter spreaders are not included here.

From Italy came these ecru runners imported by James McCutcheon. They blend beautifully with the warm tones of the old pine table and the soft, lovely finish of the silver which like that shown for the luncheon is made by Georg Jensen. Arranged in a pale wistaria-blue float, mauve tulips, fresias and yellow primulas are all in keeping with this very informal supper service.

Fresh Fruit Cup

Cream of Green Pea Soup

Cold Baked Virginia Ham

Scalloped Oysters

Baking Powder Biscuits   Iced Tea

Peach Ice Cream

Chocolate Layer Cake

As this service is very informal the fork and spoon for the dessert are placed at each cover before the meal is served. The iced tea spoon is also included, but that too can be placed when the iced tea is served and just as the supper is announced.

The glass is white etched crystal, but it could very well be a tinted glass to match the float. The china plates are unusual in shape with pretty wildflower design in lavender, pink, yellow and green. Both the long trestle table and old settle are relics from Colonial New England.

MISCELLANEOUS RECIPES EVERYONE WILL LIKE

Baking of Fruit Cakes

Fruit cakes may be baked as well as steamed and baked. They may be steamed in the oven and then baked, or steamed in a regular steamer, first covering the top of pans well with heavy waxed paper, and then put in the oven to dry out. The latter method is the one intended in Mary Lyles Wilson's recipe.

Fruit cakes may also be baked in a slow oven from three to four hours, or they may be steamed in the oven; that is, the cake pan is placed in a larger container with boiling water and baked for about five hours. The last hour of baking the container with the boiling water should be removed. In both methods the baking pan should be lined with several thicknesses of brown paper cut to fit the sides and bottom of the pan. An ordinary bread pan is excellent for this purpose.

The orange or Turkish paste called for in the recipe, page 76, may be omitted if preferred, or finely chopped candied orange peel substituted for it. The paste is quite readily purchased at any large confectioner's.

The President's Fruit Cake and Mrs. Wilson's Bride's Cake are on page 76. They were selected from the Betty Lyles Wilson Cook Book and contributed by Mary Lyles Wilson School of Cookery, Nashville, Tennessee.

Gingerbread Men

2¾ cups flour
3 teaspoons Royal Baking Powder
⅛ teaspoon salt
1 teaspoon ginger
⅔ cup molasses
⅓ cup brown sugar
1 egg
⅓ cup melted shortening

Sift flour, baking powder, salt and ginger together. Mix molasses, sugar, egg and shortening together and add the dry ingredients to make soft dough. Shape in forms of little men, animals or plain cookies; bake on greased pan in moderate oven at 375° F. ten to twelve minutes. For colored icing, see page 88.

Makes eighteen small men about four inches high.

Swedish Sand Tarts

1 cup butter
⅔ cup powdered sugar
1 egg
3 tablespoons cream
½ teaspoon almond extract
3 sweet and 1 bitter almond, grated
2 cups flour
2 teaspoons Royal Baking Powder

Wash the butter in cold water free from salt and put in cloth to press the water out. Then put it in the bowl and stir it to a cream, add the sugar slowly. Then add the whole egg, mix well and add cream, almond and almond extract and the flour which has been sifted with the baking powder. Mix to a soft dough and with floured fingers line, as thin as possible, small greased cake tins with this paste. Put on baking sheet and bake in a hot oven at 450° F. for eight minutes. Fill tarts with preserves and garnish with whipped cream.

Makes thirty tarts.

Rochester Molasses Wafers

½ cup molasses
½ cup sugar
½ cup butter
½ teaspoon cinnamon
½ teaspoon ginger
½ teaspoon soda
¾-1 cup flour

Boil all ingredients except the flour together from five to eight minutes; let it cool; then mix with sufficient flour and roll very thin. This makes a very stiff dough rather hard to roll out, but if the dough is not stiff the cookies will spread during baking.

Cut into strips one inch wide and about four inches long. Place apart on greased floured tins and bake in a moderate oven at 400° F. for six minutes. The shape is a distinctive feature.

Makes fifty wafers.

Potato Flour Puffs

2 eggs
½ teaspoon salt
1 tablespoon sugar
½ cup white potato flour or potato starch
3 teaspoons Royal Baking Powder
3 tablespoons ice water

Beat egg whites stiff and dry. Add salt and sugar to beaten yolks and fold into whites. Sift flour and baking powder twice and thoroughly beat into egg mixture. Add ice water last. Bake in greased gem pans in a moderate oven at 375° F. fifteen to twenty minutes.

Makes eight small or six large puffs.

Providence Muffins

½ cup graham flour
½ cup bran
½ teaspoon salt
2 teaspoons sugar
2 teaspoons Royal Baking Powder
1 teaspoon butter
1 tablespoon peanut butter
½ cup milk
1 egg

Mix flour, bran, salt, sugar, baking powder; melt butter and peanut butter together; add to dry mixture; add egg well beaten but not separated; add milk—beat well.

Bake in hot greased muffin tins in moderate oven at 375° F. for twelve minutes.

Makes six good sized muffins.

Ham Roulade

Cut cold baked Virginia ham into rather thin slices. Spread the following mixture on each slice very thickly. Mix one cream cheese with one-half teaspoon salt, two tablespoons fresh grated horseradish and sufficient cream to make a soft filling. Roll each up and serve on lettuce leaves with any appropriate salad or as an hors d'oeuvres.

If desired each ham roulade may be rolled in aspic, or it may be served on lettuce with aspic cut in tiny cubes.

Oyster Stew

Put four tablespoons butter into chafing-dish or deep saucepan. Heat and add one-quarter teaspoon paprika, one teaspoon salt and dash of cayenne. Put in twenty-four fresh drained oysters and cook about three minutes. Add oyster liquor and two cups rich milk or half milk and half thin cream. Cook until it boils up once and serve immediately.

Piccadillis

2 cups flour
¼ teaspoon salt
3 teaspoons Royal Baking Powder
¼ cup sugar
2 eggs
⅓ cup milk
4 tablespoons butter, melted

Mix and sift dry ingredients. Beat eggs slightly, add milk and melted butter. Add to dry ingredients and mix lightly, to make a soft dough. Divide in half. Roll out each half on floured board in a large round, 12 inches across and one-fourth inch thick. Spread with softened butter. Cut dough in fourths, and each fourth into long triangles, beginning from the center of large round. The triangles should be 1½ inches wide at edge, and about 6 inches deep. Spread each triangle with filling and roll up, beginning at wide end, so point is on top of roll. Place on greased baking sheet. Brush tops with egg yolk which has been beaten with 2 tablespoons milk. Bake in moderate oven at 400° F. for 12 minutes.

Filling

⅓ cup sugar
1½ teaspoons cinnamon
½ cup chopped nuts
1 cup seedless raisins

Mix all together.

Makes 36.

Princess Cookies

1 cup flour	½ cup butter
1 teaspoon Royal Baking Powder	½ cup almonds
	white of 1 egg

Sift flour and baking powder on kneading board. Put butter, and almonds which have been ground fine through food chopper and unbeaten white of egg on flour. Stir all ingredients thoroughly together to make a smooth paste. Roll out to about one-eighth inch thick. Cut with small cooky cutter. Spread each with white of egg and sprinkle with chopped almonds and granulated sugar. Bake in a moderate oven at 325° F. until a light brown for about eight minutes. Makes thirty cookies.

Eleventh Hour Kisses

2 egg whites	¼ teaspoon salt
¼ cup fine granulated sugar	½ teaspoon vanilla extract
½ teaspoon Royal Baking Powder	¾ cup finely cut almonds
	1 cup sliced dates

Beat egg whites until stiff but not dry; beat in sugar, one-third at a time and Royal Baking Powder. Add salt and vanilla; fold in nuts and dates; drop mixture by rounded teaspoonfuls on a well greased baking sheet or inverted pan. Bake in a slow oven at 250° F. for about thirty minutes. Cool for one minute on taking from oven. Decorate while still on the pan with a bit of candied cherry·or small pieces of citron. Remove from pan with spatula or broad-bladed knife. Makes three dozen kisses.

Date Sticks

Beat whites and yolks of two eggs separately, then beat together. Add one cup powdered sugar, two-thirds cup flour, two teaspoons Royal Baking Powder, one teaspoon vanilla extract, a little salt, one cup stoned dates, cut in pieces, and one cup broken walnut meats. Spread quite thin in a greased pan, seven inches by fourteen inches, and bake about twenty-five minutes in moderate oven at 325° F. Sprinkle with powdered sugar and cut in strips. Makes twenty date sticks.

Royal Bran Pan

1¼ cups sifted flour	¾ cup bran
4 teaspoons Royal Baking Powder	4 tablespoons shortening, melted
1 teaspoon salt	2 eggs
3 tablespoons brown sugar	¾ cup milk
	½ cup raisins, floured

Sift first four ingredients three times and add the bran. Gradually add the shortening a little at a time, stirring the dry mixture constantly. The mixture is now a crumbly mass. Beat the egg yolks well and add the milk. Add to the dry mixture. Add the raisins and beat for five minutes. Fold in stiffly beaten egg whites. Spread in a greased eight-inch square pan about three-fourths inch thick and bake in a moderate oven at 350° F. fifty to sixty minutes. Makes nine 2½-inch squares.

Cinnamon Stars

3 tablespoons butter	1 teaspoon lemon juice
1½ cups sugar	½ cup finely chopped nuts
2 whole eggs	3-3¼ cups flour
1 egg yolk	2½ teaspoons Royal Baking Powder
1 teaspoon cinnamon	¼ teaspoon salt
¼ teaspoon cloves	
¼ teaspoon nutmeg	

Cream butter, add sugar and eggs and beat very well. Add spices, lemon juice and nuts and mix well. Then add flour, sifted with baking powder and salt. Use only flour enough to make a dough that can be easily handled. Roll out very thin and cut with a star cutter or other fancy forms. Brush tops with the remaining egg white which has been beaten. Bake in moderate oven at 375° F. for ten minutes. Makes ten dozen small cookies.

Filet of Sole, Marguery

Cut English sole or flounders in small filets for serving. Put in buttered baking pan. Season with salt and pepper and sprinkle with chopped mushrooms. Cover with white wine or water and put in very slow oven and bake for about twenty minutes or until cooked through. Melt three tablespoons butter in saucepan, add three tablespoons flour. Mix and add liquor from the fish. Add six or eight fresh mussels or small oysters and about the same number cooked and shelled shrimps. Cook from three to five minutes. A very little grated Parmesan cheese can be added, if desired. Pour over fish and return to oven for about five minutes. Serve at once.

Cream of Mushroom Soup

½ pound mushrooms	1 cup rich milk
4 cups water	½ cup cream
½ small onion	few grains cayenne
1 teaspoon salt	¼ teaspoon pepper
4 tablespoons butter	paprika
4 tablespoons flour	

Save out a few of the mushroom caps to add to soup. Cover mushroom caps and stems, which have been peeled and chopped, with water. Add sliced onion and salt and boil slowly for about one-half hour. Melt butter in top of double boiler and add the mushroom caps which have been chopped. Cook about three minutes over flame. Add flour and milk to make a smooth thick sauce.

Add mushroom liquor and mushrooms rubbed through a sieve. Add cayenne, pepper, paprika and cream just before serving.

Swordfish with Lobster Sauce

Boil swordfish and cut into filets. Serve hot with the following sauce:

Finely chop one cup cooked lobster. Add to one pint milk and cook slowly over hot water for about fifteen minutes. Mix one-half tablespoon flour with water to a paste and add to milk. Stir until smooth; add two tablespoons butter and just before serving, one beaten egg, salt, pepper, paprika and one-quarter cup cream. Cook about three minutes, stirring constantly until thick and smooth.

Dumplings for Stew

Sift one cup flour with one-half teaspoon salt and three teaspoons Royal Baking Powder. Mix to a soft dough with six tablespoons milk. Drop by spoonfuls into hot stew and steam, covered, for ten minutes. Makes six dumplings.

Boo Loo Gai

From Chinese-Japanese Cook Book by Onoto Watanna and Sara Bosse. By permission of Rand McNally & Company, Publishers.

1 young chicken	1 tablespoon lard
1 tablespoon Syou Sauce or Worcestershire	1 can preserved pineapple

Singe and wash chicken and cut off all flesh. Slice in pieces convenient for serving. Heat the lard in a frying pan, being careful not to burn it, add the chicken which has been seasoned and fry until cooked through and brown, about thirty-five minutes. Add syou and pineapple cut into small pieces and cook slowly fifteen minutes longer. Remove pineapple and chicken to hot platter. Thicken gravy with one teaspoon cornstarch or two teaspoons flour. Pour over chicken and surround with hot rice. Serves six.

To Make an Excellent Breakfast Bread. Sprinkle a little cinnamon and sugar over the batter of Georgia Sally Lunn after it is in the pans and before baking.

To make Crumb or Streusel for Coffee Cakes. Use one-half as much sugar as flour and one-half as much butter as sugar.

To Avoid Scraping Carrots. Scrub carrots, then boil. When tender, rinse in cold water and the skins may be rubbed off easily, just like the skins on beets.

To Keep Sandwiches Fresh. Dip a napkin or cloth in water and wring out dry and cover sandwiches with the cloth.

To Roll Sandwiches. The day before, cut entire crust from sandwich loaf. Wrap in a damp cloth and keep in ice box or cool place. The bread will then slice and roll easily.

To Extend Sides of Cake Pan. To protect top of loaf, pin a band of heavy brown paper, well greased around outside at top of pan.

How to Beat Eggs. Beat eggs only slighly when used for a thickening agent, as in custards, puddings, sauces, etc. Beat eggs well when used to make foods light, as in sponge cakes, puffy omelets, etc.

To Cream Shortening easily. Pour a little boiling water into mixing bowl to be used. Let stand until ready to mix the cake, then empty bowl and dry, before putting in the shortening. This softens it without melting it.

For Creaming or Softening Shortening a wooden spoon is most satisfactory. It does not bend, mark the bowl or pan, nor injure the hand as a metal one often does.

Rinse all dishes having eggs, flour or milk first in cold water, then wash in hot water.

To Remove Egg Yolk from the White. If any egg yolk should get into the white when separating eggs, the whites will not beat up stiffly. Remove the yolk with a piece of the egg-shell. The edges are sharper than a spoon.

To Cook Strong Flavored Vegetables. Add one teaspoon Royal Baking Powder to cabbage, cauliflower, etc., and cook uncovered. Less odor will be noticeable.

To Cook Green Vegetables. Add one teaspoon Royal Baking Powder to each pound of vegetables; salt and cook covered in small amount of water.

To Peel Tomatoes. Pour boiling water over them, let stand one minute, then plunge into cold water. The skins will peel off quickly. Chill tomatoes thoroughly before cutting them to serve.

To Wash Spinach. Use warm water for the first washing. This loosens up much of the sand and dirt. Then wash in cool water until free from sand.

To Keep Cake Fresh. When only a small amount is eaten at a time cut the desired number of slices from center of the cake. Push the two remaining pieces close together like a whole cake, and this will keep it moist and soft for several days.

Onions peeled under water will not affect your eyes.

To Separate a Head of Lettuce. When the leaves are tightly grown together, hold under running water. The force of the water separates without breaking them.

To Keep Sliced Avocado from Discoloring, keep the pit on top of the slices until ready to serve.

To Remove Meats from Pecan Nuts easily and whole. Put them into a pan of boiling water and boil fifteen minutes. The kernels will come out whole and with very little exertion. This does not injure the flavor of the nuts.

To Cut Marshmallows and Dried Fruits such as raisins, dates, etc., use floured scissors.

To Separate Seeded Raisins. Wash whole package under cold water faucet and they will come apart readily.

To Prevent Nuts and Fruits from Sinking in Cake. Heat before rolling in flour and adding to cake batter.

To Blanch Almonds. After shelling, place in boiling water and let boil one or two minutes. Drain; then skins can be easily removed. If not in hurry let almonds stay in cold water over night, pour off water and same results will be obtained.

To Prevent Filling from Soaking in Pie Crust. Dust over bottom crust with a mixture of flour and sugar before adding fruit or other filling.

To Cut Very Fresh Bread Easily. Heat the knife, which should be sharp.

To Easily Remove Paraffin from jellies and jams, place a narrow tape or string, long enough to extend beyond the jar, across top before pouring on hot paraffin. This will enable you to easily remove and replace it.

To Use Cocoa in Place of Chocolate. Use three and one-half tablespoons cocoa for each square or ounce of chocolate, and add one-half tablespoon butter.

To Whip Cream. Use heavy cream for whipping and have it thoroughly chilled. Whip with rotary egg beater or cream whipper. Whip until cream begins to stiffen (if beaten too long, it will turn to butter), then add sugar if it is to be sweetened. Add one tablespoon powdered sugar and one-half teaspoon vanilla extract to each cup (one-half pint) of cream. Continue to whip until cream holds its shape. Heavy cream about doubles in bulk when whipped.

To Cut the Birthday Cake Into Sufficient Pieces. With a sharp pointed knife start at the outside edge of cake and cut around in circles to the center, then slice through each circular piece as illustrated.